MW00487419

RIGHT TO COUNSEL

A Lawyer's Struggle to Defend a Serial Killer

Bertha —

Best Wishes To one of our FAVORITE MoTHER-IN-LAWS !!

JAMES WILLIAM POTTS

Go "STINS"

8/2008

SPHINX® PUBLISHING
AN IMPRINT OF SOURCEBOOKS, INC.®
NAPERVILLE, ILLINOIS
www.SphinxLegal.com

Published by: **Sphinx® Publishing, An Imprint of Sourcebooks, Inc.®**
Naperville Office
P.O. Box 4410
Naperville, Illinois 60567-4410
(630) 961-3900
Fax: 630-961-2168
www.sourcebooks.com
www.SphinxLegal.com

This publication is designed to provide accurate and authoritative information in
regard to the subject matter covered. It is sold with the understanding that the
publisher is not engaged in rendering legal, accounting, or other professional
service. If legal advice or other expert assistance is required, the services of a
competent professional person should be sought.

*From a Declaration of Principles Jointly Adopted by a Committee of the
American Bar Association and a Committee of Publishers and Associations*

This product is not a substitute for legal advice.

Disclaimer required by Texas statutes.

Library of Congress Cataloging-in-Publication Data

Potts, James William.
  Right to counsel : a lawyer's struggle to defend a serial killer / by James
William Potts.
    p. cm.
  ISBN 978-1-57248-669-0 (pbk. : alk. paper) 1. Potts, James William. 2.
Lawyers--United States--Biography. 3. Public defenders--California--Marin
County. 4. Capital punishment--California--Marin County. 5. Death row--
California--Marin county. 6. Mattson, Michael Dee--Trial, litigation, etc. 7.
Serial murderers--California--Marin County--Biography. 8. Trials (Murder)--
California--Marin County. I. Title.
KF373.A3P68 2008
345.73'056--dc22
                                    2008020341

Printed and bound in the United States of America.
VP 10 9 8 7 6 5 4 3 2 1

This book is dedicated to my wife Brenda, who has been, and continues to be, my best friend and the biggest supporter of my dreams and pursuits.

To my sons Jamal and Jamayne and my stepson Zaylore, who are my inspiration to move ever forward. The love and bond we share is undaunted and unconditional.

Acknowledgments

To Monique R. High, my agent, editor, and book shrink, who has taken my raw material and helped me shape it into a masterful piece of work.

To Susan Chin (editing) and Vanessa Mabourakh (marketing), two excellent contributors to the WriteHigh Literary Agency staff, who were directly responsible for the completion and sale of this book.

To Ronald S. Smith, Attorney-at-Law, who, as a mentor and friend, continues to be a champion for the underdog.

To Detective Pat Dingle (retired), who has assisted me with insightful details of interactions between himself and Michael Dee Mattson.

To my wife, Brenda Cameron-Potts, who stood by my side throughout the many hours of writing and editing.

To Shawn McGahey Webb, Deputy Attorney General, State of California, Department of Justice, for her assistance in obtaining copies of the transcripts from each trial.

In addition, I would like to thank Erin Shanahan, Esq., Sphinx Managing Editor, and Dominique Raccah, the Publisher of Sourcebooks, Inc., for believing in this book.

Foreword

The Fifth and Sixth Amendments to the Constitution guarantee the right against self-incrimination, the right to remain silent, and the right to counsel, along with other trial-related rights. When faced with media reports of brutal crimes, especially those against children, heated emotions get the better of us, and we often forget that these rights are afforded to every accused individual. Defense attorneys who represent suspects accused of such felonies are often looked upon with disdain, even though legal ethics do not allow them to withdraw from the representation of a defendant just because they may find the subject matter personally repugnant. Every defendant—every accused man or woman under the law—has the right to counsel under the United States Constitution, no matter what he or she is purported to have done, or to whom.

CONTENTS

Michael Dee Mattson's Mug Shot

INTRODUCTION

In July 1982 Michael Dee Mattson was on San Quentin's death row, convicted of the kidnapping, rape, and murder of several young girls in California. As with every death row inmate, he had been granted an automatic appeal to the California Supreme Court. A cold, calculating sexual predator, who showed no signs of remorse for his crimes nor of having been rehabilitated in prison, he had recourse to an adolescence of sexual ambiguity to bolster his appeal— Mattson's mother would say that, as a child, he stole women's clothing and underwear to wear himself. He claimed that he had been diagnosed as suffering from schizophrenia, attributed to major traumatic childhood experiences. Expert testimony expressed that the deprivation and abuse he had undergone as a child, as well as a history of sexual identity problems—a vacillation between male and female orientation—had led him to cross-dressing and drug abuse, contributing to his depravity.

As a law clerk, I became personally involved with Mattson's case. My law professor asked me to assist him in representing a death row client whose appeal he had been assigned to. Knowing nothing of the case, I could not anticipate the tug-of-war that would take place between my personal and professional principles once I learned what crimes Mattson had been convicted of committing. And so, I eagerly accepted the assignment, only to quickly find out that our new client had been convicted of the kidnapping, rape, and murder of several young women and girls, some mere children.

The subject matter touched me particularly deeply because my only sister had been assaulted three years earlier by a sexual predator. Could I go through with this assignment? I decided I had to. But then, adding to fate's cruel sense of humor, it was I who ultimately found the issue resulting in the reversal of Mattson's conviction, a fact that caused a tremendous amount of stress between my wife and me. Throughout the appeals process, she remained vehemently opposed to my helping Mattson in any manner. The strength of our marital bond was tested on more than one occasion as I worked on the case.

Prior to my involvement in this case, my life had been uncomplicated. I'd been happily married, with one young child and another on the way. Approaching my last year of law school, I had a bright future on the horizon. I had passed through the fire and emerged forged. After my participation in the case, my career path took me away from criminal law. I began working with employers to help ensure that their respective working environments are without discriminatory practices both on the state and federal levels. It has been a rewarding experience.

As the years have passed, sexual predators like Mattson have continued to stalk, kidnap, rape, and murder our children. Families of victims and communities across the country have had to deal with the murders of young girls like Samantha Runion, Jessica Lunsford, Sarah Michelle Lunde, Amanda Brown, JonBenet Ramsey, and Cherise Iverson. All of these girls were brutally assaulted and subsequently murdered by individuals fitting a similar profile to that of Michael Dee Mattson. Society wants this type of predator held accountable on a national and international front.

Yet, as citizens, we have to remember—we can never forget—that in our search for vindication, justice must be served in a manner consistent with state and federal laws so as not to diminish the rights of every citizen of the United States. If we extinguish those rights, the rights of the victims to have their killers answer for their crimes will be lost as well. Vigilante justice has no place in American society. I am just as adamant that the legal system we have in place not be daunted by sloppy police work or emotional, knee-jerk reactions that ultimately destroy the basic foundations of the Constitution.

But I was not always like this. My personal ethics once clashed with my professional principles and responsibilities. When all was said and done, however, I learned that having the mental discipline to make the hard choices life offers up is the only way to survive unencumbered by its challenges.

ONE

THE CRIMES

It was July of 1978 in Los Angeles—a time for picnics, treks to amusement parks, couples exchanging marital vows, and, unfortunately for some families, a summer that ultimately brought the type of pain that no parent should ever have to endure. Unbeknownst to my wife Betty and me, it was a summer we would never be able to forget.

We were expecting our second child. We found the prospect of adding to our family exciting, but it was overshadowed by a complicated pregnancy that kept Betty confined to the house. Adding to her discomfort was a very hot summer and a husband working full-time while attending law school five nights a week, year-round. Unfortunately, my schedule left very little time for Betty and me to be together. Between my schedule and the emotions of pregnancy, she constantly admonished me to spend more time with her. The pressure was enormous for a 27-year-old man—working a full-time job; trying to get an education that ultimately might create a lifestyle most people dream about, but that also required endless hours of study; a complicated pregnancy; Saturdays at the library; and, a wife making demands that felt somewhat unrealistic under the circumstances.

———◦◦———

Unbeknownst to us that summer, Michael Dee Mattson—a name that would become too familiar to us in time—was on parole from an Oregon state prison. The reason for his stint in prison: On August 1, 1971, while hitchhiking, Mattson was picked up by a teenage girl, Jeanette Kors, and her brother Joe. He pulled a knife on the pair, ordered Joe out of the vehicle while they were parked on the side of the road, and kidnapped, raped, and robbed Jeanette off the main highway. Later that same day, Mattson was captured while driving Jeanette's car. At the time, he was just shy of his 18th birthday. Following his conviction and subsequent two-year incarceration, apparently already planning on committing more crimes, Mattson vowed he would kill all his future victims to prevent any of them from testifying against him. By 1978 Mattson had returned to Southern California and taken up residence in nearby La Mirada.

———◦◦———

One late Saturday afternoon that summer, after spending another eight-hour day at the library, I cut my study time short and headed home, hoping to spend some time with my wife. I found Betty, a small-framed woman with dark-brown hair, glasses, and a light-skinned complexion that denoted her Louisiana heritage, in the bedroom, and I could see that she was upset. On the screen of our fifteen-inch television was a newscaster reporting on a 9-year-old girl who had gone missing from a local pool. While I wondered what kind of human being would kidnap a 9-year-old girl, I felt lucky that it did not affect us personally. Unfortunately, I did not realize the effect this kidnapping would have on our lives after all.

———◦◦———

Michael Dee Mattson's first victim after his release from prison was 9-year-old Cheryl Kristy Gutierrez, who disappeared at approximately 4:00 p.m. on August 11, 1978, from the parking lot of Santa Fe Springs High School. Cheryl had been swimming in a public pool with her sisters, 12-year-old Sylvia and 5-year-old Toni. The girls were only one mile from their home. Cheryl and Sylvia had an argument over what time they should finish swimming. Cheryl wanted to go home earlier than Sylvia, so she left the pool area, angry and upset. Sylvia, thinking Cheryl had gone to call their mother from the pay phone outside the pool to pick her up, was not concerned. The last time her sisters saw her, Cheryl was wearing only a two-piece, floral bathing suit, a pair of flip-flops, and was carrying a white beach towel.

Approximately thirty minutes later, their mother, Esther Gutierrez, arrived to pick them up at the prearranged time. She had never received a phone call from Cheryl. After a brief conversation with her oldest daughter, Esther and Sylvia looked for Cheryl for two anguished hours, without success.

One witness, Robert Stumpf, the foreman in charge of the buildings and maintenance of the high school, remembered seeing a young Hispanic girl waiting near the parking lot entrance when he left to go home around 3:30 that afternoon. He later recalled also seeing a young man with long dark hair and a beard sitting in a yellow car with large black tires, a black top, and a lot of mud on the passenger side door. The vehicle was parked within just a few yards of the young girl.

Growing even more concerned that they could not find Cheryl, the Gutierrez family called the Los Angeles County Sheriff's Norwalk station to report that Cheryl was missing. A description of Cheryl—four feet tall, sixty-five pounds, with long black hair, and wearing the clothes described—was immediately dispatched over the radio to all local law enforcement agencies.

A search party—consisting of twelve sheriff's deputies, fifteen Explorer Scouts, and a helicopter equipped with a bullhorn repeatedly announcing the search for Cheryl—was immediately dispatched.

By the following day, the search party expanded into a wider area. The clock was ticking and hope that Cheryl would be found alive was quickly running out. Sergeant Tim McGraw of the Los Angeles County

Sheriff's Department supervised the search from the front yard of the Gutierrez family home. McGraw had the search parties going door-to-door, to empty lots, neighborhood buildings, and any other place he could think of where a child might be found. Every volunteer was hoping for the best but thinking the worst as time began to take its emotional toll.

At approximately 6:30 that evening, picnickers at Legg Lake in Whittier Narrows Recreation Area off the 605 Freeway discovered the body of a young girl. The location of the corpse was approximately seven miles north-northeast of where Cheryl was last seen alive. Deputy Ronald Riordan and his partner, Deputy Stewart Reed, were dispatched to the location.

Under the overgrown shrubbery lay the naked body of a small girl splayed facedown in the bushes. The top of a two-piece floral swimming suit was wrapped tightly around her neck, along with a piece of monofilament fishing line and a handy wipe.

Every hope for a rescue faded quickly, and the harsh reality set firmly in place. A person or persons unknown took Cheryl's young life. The sheriff's department quickly ruled out any connection with the

Hillside Strangler, another case that was being investigated at the same time that involved the murders of thirteen young girls and women in the Los Angeles area between September 1977 and February 1978.

———◦———

When the news that Cheryl had been found murdered and that her killer was still at large hit the morning paper, my thoughts turned inward as I remembered how I felt when my own sister was raped and my subsequent gun-toting search for the man who violated her. Luckily for both of us, I never found him.

Looking at my pregnant wife and thinking of our son, I thought of how parents coach their children never to speak to strangers or get into vehicles with people they do not know. Schools reinforce these same safeguards over and over again, and even the media in movies and television programs depict scenarios for instructive purposes. Yet no matter how many precautions we take, there's always a chance that our children could be lured into the trap of a predator like Mattson.

———◦———

A few days later, Dr. Joan Shipley of the Coroner's Office subsequently confirmed that Cheryl died from asphyxiation due to ligature strangulation and/or suffocation. Dr. Shipley found bleeding under Cheryl's skin between the skin and the bones of her scalp, which was consistent with a blow being struck. Additionally, Cheryl's hymen was lacerated. Dr. Shipley officially ruled Cheryl's death a homicide. The hunt for Cheryl's killer was launched.

The Los Angeles County Sheriff's Department, in trying to piece together the events surrounding Cheryl's murder, asked the public for help with any facts that could lead to the capture of the individual or individuals responsible. The case was assigned to Detective Stuart Reed, one of the two deputies first dispatched to the crime scene. As time would tell, Reed was about to embark on a trail for a ruthless, vicious killer who preyed on young girls and expressed a total disregard for human life.

———◆———

As Betty and I continued with our daily routine of caring for our son Jamal and preparing for the impending birth of our new baby and for me to officially become a lawyer, Mattson, then 24, established his own modus operandi. While we were planning our life, Mattson was taking others.

On the morning of July 20, 16-year-old Deanna Musquiz, excited to learn how to drive and obtain her driver's license, left her home in Hemet, a small town in Riverside County, at approximately 9:30 in the morning to attend a driving lesson that was supposed to begin thirty minutes later. A call from Deanna's driving instructor complaining that she failed to show up for her appointment prompted an immediate search by her family, as it was unlike Deanna to be so irresponsible. Unfortunately, at 7:10 that evening, after only a few hours of searching, Deanna Musquiz was found murdered.

Her death was investigated by Detective Howard C. Rush of the Hemet Police Department. Her body, which appeared to have been lifeless for approximately ten hours, was found in the Hemet area. She was nude and appeared to have been raped. Her blouse was wrapped tightly around her neck and tied in place. Her pants were found nearby.

F. Rene Modgelin, a physician and pathologist working for the County of Riverside, examined the body the next day. He determined that she was murdered before 2:30 p.m. on the previous day. She had been raped and strangled. The search began for her killer or killers, as well.

———◆———

Months later, Mattson confessed to the murder of Deanna Musquiz, but later recanted any knowledge of her death and successfully argued and proved that he was at work at the alleged time of the murder. Contrary evidence would later be presented that Mattson knew specific details about the victim, the means of death, and the location of the body that only the killer could have known, since the exact specifics of Deanna's murder were never printed in the newspaper. Yet, unfortunately for Deanna's family, her murder would never officially be put to rest, and Mattson would not be held accountable for her death. Unofficially, though, we can safely surmise that Mattson, in all likelihood, did murder Deanna.

———◆———

Mattson's next victim was Adele Jean Corradini, a 16-year-old girl last seen by her mother at 8:30 in the morning on September 6. Adele's mother, Jo Ann Corradini, dropped her off on a local street corner where the teenager expected to be picked up by friends and be given a ride to her part-time job as a chambermaid at a motel in Dana Point, a small seaside community in Orange County. Adele was last seen wearing a delicate white eyelet blouse with straps, a hooded multicolored sweater, denim jeans, and blue tennis shoes. Around her neck she wore a puka-shell necklace. Unfortunately, Adele never made it to her shift at the motel that day.

The Corradini family received no word on Adele's whereabouts for eight agonizing weeks. Then, on November 9, Adele's remains were finally located in a wooded area in Duarte, above the 210 and 605 freeways. She was found by Lieutenant Barry A. Fitzgerald of the Los Angeles County Sheriff's Department, but her body was no longer intact. After two months of being exposed to the elements, it was badly decomposed and missing the right leg. Because of the condition of the corpse, the cause of death could never be officially determined. On the skeletonized remains, however, were a puka-shell necklace, a small, gold, flexible ring made with an S-shaped link, a white eyelet blouse, and a single blue tennis shoe. No underwear was found on or near the body. Adele's mother used the pieces of jewelry to identify her daughter's remains.

Unlike Cheryl Gutierrez, however, Adele's remains were not accidentally discovered. Detective Reed, acting on a tip from another detective, Detective Pat Dingle of the North Las Vegas Police Department, went to North Las Vegas, Nevada, to interrogate Mattson, who, at the time, was a Nevada suspect in a similar crime. While interviewing Mattson, Reed obtained critical information from him about exactly where the body of Adele could be located. Operating on these directions, Detective Reed telephoned Lieutenant Fitzgerald and pointed him to the remains in Duarte. Additionally, Mattson also volunteered information about the killing. He told Reed that he had picked up a 16-year-old girl hitchhiking in the area, and had taken her to a remote part of Duarte off the Foothill Freeway, raped her three times, and then strangled her.

———◆———

Kiz Rene Livingston, a 15-year-old resident of Seal Beach, was Mattson's final California victim in 1978. Kiz, heading to Huntington Beach, missed her bus, so she decided to hitchhike along the Pacific Coast Highway. It was approximately 8:30 a.m. when Mattson picked her up in his yellow Plymouth Duster and offered to take her wherever she wanted to go. Kiz told Mattson her intended destination on Lake Street in Huntington Beach. However, before reaching the address, Mattson made a sudden U-turn and ordered Kiz to lock the passenger-side door. He hit Kiz across the face, which made her start to cry. Mattson began to scream at her, ordering her to stop, while continuing to slap her over and over again. He did not want other people to become suspicious. He finally told her that if she did not "shut up," he would kill her. He placed a knife by her thigh and told her not to make any more movements that would attract the attention of people passing by.

Mattson, driving north on the 605 Freeway, pulled over by the Carson Street exit, where he got out of the car because he had to urinate. The whole time he was driving, Mattson was drinking Budweiser from a Styrofoam cup. While Mattson was relieving himself,

Kiz took the opportunity to try to escape. She got out of the car and walked very quickly toward the off ramp. Mattson saw what she was trying to do, and immediately chased her down and grabbed her roughly by the arm. Mattson apologized to her and threw away the knife in the ivy by the side of the road. He promised Kiz he would take her home, and led her back to the Plymouth, only to find that he could not get the car to start. Mattson got out of the car and walked to a callbox to phone a tow truck. After a while the truck arrived and gave Mattson's car a jumpstart. Kiz, throughout the process, never made any attempt to speak with the tow-truck driver. She may have been in shock, too terrified Mattson would kill her to speak.

Mattson got back into the car and once again promised Kiz that he would take her home. He started driving, and after a while, Kiz told him that they were going in the wrong direction. Mattson insisted that they were driving the right way. But instead of driving her home as he had promised, Mattson drove her to the Diamond Bar area, finally pulling over on Pathfinder Road—a dirt roadway with no sidewalks or curbs. Mattson told Kiz that he had to urinate again and left the car, leaving it running this time. Upon his return, he turned off the car and forced Kiz out of the vehicle and down a steep hill to a secluded area.

He ordered the young girl to take off certain parts of her clothing and beat her when she tried to refuse. In his fury, Mattson ripped off her garments himself. Then he proceeded to brutally rape and sodomize her, while she cried and begged him to stop.

When Mattson was finally finished with her, he contemplated his next move. The act was done. The sexual fantasy of the encounter was over. What to do next? Mattson finally decided that he could not kill her, and drove her to her girlfriend's house. Mattson was later quoted as stating that the reason he did not murder Kiz was because "he could not find a rock big enough to bash her head in."

———◈———

After leaving Kiz alive that day, Mattson seemed to be concerned that he made a mistake in not killing her. As in the case of Jeanette Kors, leaving Kiz alive could eventually cost him his freedom. Shortly after he gave

Kiz a reprieve from death, Mattson fled California and found his way to Nevada.

Once again falling prey to his demons, on September 20, Mattson struck again. This time his victim was Sonia Lindsey, a 20-year-old African American student at North Las Vegas Community College. One evening, as she was returning from class, Sonia got into her car, which was parked in the college parking lot, and was startled when Mattson aggressively pushed himself into the car after her. He demanded money and drove her into the desert, where he subsequently raped and sodomized her. Fortunately, Sonia was able to escape when Mattson drove them back into Las Vegas to get gas. Along with Kiz, Sonia was one of the lucky ones to survive Mattson's 1978 crime spree. No other survivors besides Kiz and Sonia ever came to light.

TWO

CAPTURE

It all began with a telephone call from the station dispatcher at approximately 1:00 a.m. on September 21, 1978. Patrick "Pat" Dingle, 32, a detective with the North Las Vegas Police Department since the young age of 24, was responsible for investigating major crimes in North Las Vegas. He was a tall, lean man who had seen his share of action over the last decade and a half as an undercover narcotics agent for the Office of Navel Intelligence, through three tours in Vietnam rescuing downed pilots, and finally as a police officer with a distinguished career fighting organized crime. To be called that early in the morning, he knew it had to be something serious. The dispatcher told him that a student from the local community college had been kidnapped, raped, and sodomized. Incredibly, she had escaped from her assailant, who drove off in her car, and was at the station reporting the incident. Her name was Sonia Lindsey.

After obtaining the basic details of the incident, Dingle got dressed quickly and drove over to the campus parking lot to visually investigate the scene of the kidnapping. Upon his arrival, he spotted a yellow Plymouth Duster that looked like it had been in its fair share of fender benders. It was the only car in Dingle's view. A closer inspection of the vehicle and its interior only produced an array of women's clothing, but nothing that openly suggested to him that the car had any particular association with the crime he was investigating. As the senior detective for the North Las Vegas Police Department, though, Dingle trusted his professional skills and experience, and decided to run the license plate. On his handheld radio, he called into the dispatcher and gave him the pertinent information. After a few moments of silence, the dispatcher's voice broke the silence of the darkness. He informed Dingle that the plate number returned to a "Michael Dee Mattson of La Mirada, California." Dingle acknowledged the dispatcher with the recognized 10-4 code, checked his watch, and realized that it was still too early in the morning to call the La Mirada Police Department.

There was a chill that night, and Dingle zipped up his jacket all the way while he took a casual stroll around the area, searching for anything that would give him any additional information about his investigation. Satisfied that he had not overlooked anything in the parking area, he took one more look at the interior of the Plymouth. Not seeing anything new to note, Dingle returned to his vehicle and drove to the station.

The police station was almost empty when Dingle arrived that morning. After a brief conversation with the watch commander, Dingle learned that Sonia had been taken to the hospital for a medical examination, and Dingle was handed a copy of the report of the incident as described by the unfortunate victim.

On his way to his office, Dingle stopped by the kitchenette to get a cup of coffee, but was dismayed to find the pot empty. He cursed under his breath and made a fresh pot. While waiting for the coffee to brew, he found a spot at the small table in the precinct kitchen, setting aside the cigarette butt–filled ashtray and a day-old newspaper. After making himself relatively comfortable, he slowly read the report, trying to make sure he burned every detail into his memory. Without taking his eyes off the report, he pulled a cigarette from the pack in his shirt pocket and lit it mechanically. This wasn't the first of these types of reports he had read during his years on the force.

Later that morning, Dingle was still trying to put together the pieces of the puzzle from the night before. Having smoked more Camel cigarettes than he would have liked, and slugged down more coffee than his stomach appreciated, Dingle suddenly realized that the morning had crept up on him and that he could finally call the La Mirada Police Department about the car he found in the parking lot the night before.

Soon, not only did he confirm that the owner of the vehicle in question was indeed Michael Dee Mattson, but he also learned that Mattson had a prior conviction in Oregon for the same type of crime as the case Dingle was working on. Dingle was convinced he had a major suspect for his case. Everything tied in, and his long night at the precinct produced the required results.

Satisfied that he had done all of his due diligence, he sprung into action. Having previously ordered his department to send out a teletype to the western United States, including a description of the victim's car, he updated the information with an "attempt to locate one Michael Dee Mattson for kidnapping and rape."

Dingle checked his watch. The time reflected what his body was telling him. He had hardly slept over the last twenty-four hours, and he was starting to struggle to stay awake and productive. He gave up and slowly rose to his feet, exited his office, and informed the dispatcher that he was heading home for some much needed rest.

The next day, September 22, Dingle returned to his desk at the precinct to review his notes on the case. The watch commander called him to report that the victim's car had been located approximately thirty miles north-northeast of North Las Vegas on Highway 93 by Pioche, a small rural town. A lucky break for sure. And adding to that luck, Dingle would later learn, was a heads-up play by Archie Robinson, sheriff of White Pine County, Nevada. Robinson was an old-time country sheriff with a cowboy accent and attitude. His patrol area encompassed played-out mines and working ranches. Robinson, while sitting in his office in Ely, Nevada, read the teletype sent out by Dingle's office. Robinson remembered that a family of Mattsons lived some distance away in a backwoods area called Cherry Creek. And so, on a hunch, the sheriff decided to drive out there to talk to the family and see if they were the same Mattsons Dingle was looking for.

After a long drive over the rural roads, Robinson arrived at the Mattson home and gently knocked on the front door. An elderly man, his wife in the background, answered the door and was visibly surprised to see the sheriff.

"Mornin' folks, sorry to disturb you so early."

"No problem, Sheriff. How can we help you?" the elderly man responded.

"Well, sir, by any chance, do you know a Michael Mattson?"

The elderly man's expression of disgust signaled to the sheriff that he was at the right place.

"Yeah, we know him. He's our grandson. What's he done now?"

"Well, Mr. Mattson, maybe nothing. Have you seen him?"

Mrs. Mattson, possibly recognizing the seriousness of the situation with the sheriff standing at her front door first thing in the morning, responded in a tired voice, "He's here, sleepin' in the guest room. I'll get 'im."

The sheriff was surprised to hear that the young man he was looking for was actually asleep inside the house at that very moment. Michael, awakened by his grandparents, shuffled to the front door and was met by Robinson. His grandparents could only watch, openmouthed, as Robinson immediately took Mattson into custody. When Robinson arrested him, Mattson was informed that he was a suspect in the kidnapping and sexual assault of a college student that took place two days earlier. Robinson also advised Mattson of his Miranda rights and specifically told him that he had the right to remain silent, that anything he said could be used against him in court, that he had the right to consult with an attorney and have one present while being questioned, and that an attorney would be appointed for him by the court before any questioning took place if he wanted one. Mattson acknowledged that he understood his rights, but Robinson did not question him and Mattson did not volunteer any information about the offenses that he was being charged with at that time, nor did he ask for a lawyer.

While he was being booked at the station, Mattson casually asked Robinson how he had been identified. Robinson told Mattson that the victim had given detailed information regarding his identification, including some tattoos she saw on Mattson's arms. In response, Mattson replied, "I didn't think she saw those." Mattson did not say anything else to the sheriff. Robinson did not tell Mattson of any of the additional evidence that ultimately led him to the home of Mattson's grandparents in Cherry Creek.

At last, Mattson was in police custody and off the streets. In the relatively short period of time he had been out of prison, he had repeatedly kidnapped, raped, and murdered without hesitation or mercy. His victims were all young girls who could not defend themselves against his size and strength.

Robinson, after processing Mattson, contacted Dingle to tell him that he had his boy in custody. Dingle was elated that his prime suspect had been captured so quickly and without any violence or anyone else being hurt.

On September 25, Detective Pat Dingle and his partner, Bob King, drove to Ely to bring the suspect back to North Las Vegas. The three-hour drive went by quickly as their anticipation and excitement of seeing and picking up Mattson grew. Although both men were internally excited, on this trip they were all business. They were both professionals who understood that there was a chance Mattson was not the right man.

Upon their arrival, they met with Robinson to officially take over custody of Mattson. The sheriff led them down to the holding cells on the lower level of the building. With every step Dingle's heart pounded a little harder. With all his years of experience, solving this particular crime gave him an adrenalin rush he did not feel in most cases.

As the three officials entered the holding area, Mattson, the only prisoner in the cell, rose to his feet. The minute Dingle set eyes on the prisoner, the hairs on the back of his neck stood up—he literally recoiled and could not hide the instinctive physical repulsion he felt for Mattson. His first impression of Mattson in his six-by-six gray-walled jail cell reminded him of Charles Manson who, nine years earlier, had master-minded the murder of actress Sharon Tate and her guests in a shockingly gruesome manner.

Mattson represented everything contrary to the morals of a high-principled detective like Dingle. Dingle abhored senseless killing and became a crime fighter while serving in the Navy in the late 1960s. As an undercover naval narcotics agent, Dingle was sent to Southern California to work on drug cases. When things grew too hot for him there, the Navy pulled him out and sent him to Vietnam, where he and his team rescued 134 pilots shot down over North Vietnam. Following his honorable discharge from the Navy, and the day before his 21st birthday, he joined the North Las Vegas Police Department, where he made detective by the age of 24, a just reward for his tenacity and wealth of experience.

Outside Mattson's holding cell, at 32 and face-to-face with his prisoner, Dingle put his personal feelings aside and calmly advised Mattson of his Miranda rights—the right to remain silent and be represented by an attorney.

Peering back at Dingle through the bars of the cell, Mattson inched forward, placed both hands on the bars, and said in a hoarse whisper, "I understand my rights." The sheepish grin slowly faded from Mattson's face as he looked into Dingle's eyes and understood how serious the detective was. At this point he asked for an attorney.

Dingle and King took Mattson from the holding cell in Ely and drove him the three hours to the North Las Vegas Police Department without asking him any questions about the case. Upon arrival, he was officially booked as the main suspect in the kidnapping and brutal rape of Sonia Lindsey.

The next morning, September 26, Dingle received a call from Detective Branch of the Huntington Beach Police Department in Southern California. Branch was investigating the kidnapping and rape of Kiz Livingston, and he called Dingle because he was interested in learning the facts and details of the North Las Vegas kidnapping and rape of Sonia Lindsey to see how close the similarities to his case actually were, hoping that the man Dingle had in custody was the same perpetrator he was looking for. It would make his job easier if the guilty person was already in custody at another precinct. He began with polite small talk before getting around to the real reason he called. For a successful police detective, Branch was a soft-spoken individual and Dingle had to press the phone closer against his ear to hear him more clearly.

After discussing the specifics of the crimes in great detail, Branch became satisfied that there were several similarities between the crimes committed against Kiz and Sonia, and that the descriptions of the man were similar and matched the description of Mattson. Branch had Dingle send him copies of his report on Mattson, along with Mattson's fingerprints and mug shot. While the detectives could not have realized it at the time, they were one step closer to solving a large number of murders in California and stopping a serial killer.

Later in the day, Mattson was placed in a lineup, standing shoulder-to-shoulder with similar-looking individuals, including other prisoners. Standing on the other side of a two-way mirror, shielded from the view of Mattson, was Mattson's court-appointed lawyer, Deputy Public Defender Gubler, as well as a deputy district attorney from the District Attorney's Office who would be prosecuting Mattson. After being told that she would not be seen behind the two-way mirror, a nervous-looking Sonia Lindsey was brought into the room with the two attorneys, and she immediately picked out Mattson as her assailant.

As the jailer escorted all the lineup participants back to their respective jail cells, Mattson was led past Dingle's office and made eye contact with him. They both nodded politely at each other.

"Hey, Jailer, I wanna talk to Dingle," Mattson said before he entered his cell.

"'Bout what?" the jailer asked.

"That's between him and me," Mattson answered.

"Well, he's gonna want to know why!"

When Mattson was nonresponsive, the guard took Mattson by his arm and led him into his cell. Being a high-profile suspect, Mattson was kept in a cell by himself instead of in the general holding cell where most of the prisoners were held until they were either released or sent to prison.

Twenty minutes later, the jailer informed Dingle of Mattson's request. Dingle was somewhat surprised. The Nevada case against Mattson was already wrapped up. Dingle had everything he needed to close the case, including the suspect's background, and a positive identification by the victim. But Dingle made the decision to speak with Mattson knowing that if he was able to procure a confession from Mattson, that would be the final nail in Mattson's coffin. However, Dingle knew that he had to be cautious about his attitude when he spoke with Mattson. After all, he had over-reacted earlier when he exposed his feelings of repulsion to Mattson the first time they met. This was a mistake he did not intend to repeat.

Dingle had the jailer take Mattson from his cell to an interrogation room. In the interrogation room, there was a battered-looking table with four chairs surrounding it in the center of the room. The walls were made out of the same cinderblocks as the cells, painted over in a thick layer of dingy gray paint. A single light bulb hung down from the ceiling just above the center of the table, leaving the corners of the room in shadows. The guard handcuffed Mattson to the table so he could not attack Dingle and left him alone in the room.

In anxious anticipation, Dingle headed off in the direction of the interrogation room. Upon his arrival, he marshaled his feelings, for he knew he would have to finesse Mattson to get a confession out of him. He could not show Mattson the hatred and disgust he actually felt toward him.

Dingle once again read Mattson his rights, making it very clear that Mattson did not have to speak with him at all and that if Mattson wanted to speak with Dingle anyway, he was allowed to have his attorney with him in the room.

"Oh, I understand my rights, Detective."

"That's good, Michael, but do you choose to waive your rights and speak to me without the presence of an attorney?" Dingle asked Mattson.

"Yeah, I do," Mattson replied. "But alls I really want to know is what happened to my car. Where is it?"

The mood of the moment was very relaxed. Dingle told Mattson that his Plymouth Duster was safe and in the police impound lot, and he asked him who owned the clothes that were found inside. Mattson smugly replied that the clothes were his, including the female attire.

His eyebrows raised, Dingle further inquired, "The *female* clothes I found in your car are *yours,* Michael?"

With a smirk on his face, Mattson replied, "Yep."

"Care to explain that last answer?" Dingle remarked with a grin.

"Well, if you ever speak with my mother, you can ask her."

In the course of their short conversation, Mattson also nervously asked Dingle whether the Nevada kidnapping and rape victim had identified him. Dingle said that she had. Seeming almost relieved, the suspect proceeded to tell Dingle about the kidnapping and rape in his own words. The discussion became more conversational in tone than a usual interrogation, both men leaning forward and drinking cups of coffee. Mattson, possibly sensing the mood shift, told Dingle that he needed psychiatric attention and wanted help for his "deviant sexual behavior."

"Michael, although I personally believe counseling might be beneficial for you, that is simply not my call. However, because you have requested to see a doctor, I will make the arrangements."

Following his conversation with Mattson, Dingle placed a call to Mattson's mother, Jackie Mattson Golyer, in California, to find out if Mattson was telling the truth about the women's clothing found in his car. Mattson's mother told Dingle that Mattson was a transvestite, who, since his early childhood, had stolen and kept women's clothes, primarily underwear, for his own use. Mattson's mother was a soft-spoken woman who, by the tone and demeanor of her voice, seemed to have resigned herself to her son's fate. Dingle also followed up on Mattson's request to see a doctor.

Later, Mattson alleged that Dingle used psychological coercion and the promise of counseling as a way to elicit his admissions and confessions without the presence of counsel. Dingle would contend that at the time of the interview and to the best of his knowledge, no attorney had been appointed to represent Mattson. In fact, at the initial lineup when Sonia identified Mattson as her abductor and rapist, Deputy Public Defender Gubler never stated that he represented Mattson or any of the other lineup participants. However, as the facts would later reveal, Gubler did sign his name on the lineup form above a printed statement that read: "Signature of Public Defender or attorney for suspect." Indeed, before the lineup was conducted, Gubler spoke to the group of participants and told them that he was there as counsel for Mattson, the suspect, and they should all cooperate so that the lineup could be fair. Of particular note, though, is that Gubler never had any personal, individual contact with Mattson and did not take any responsibility to advise, counsel, or otherwise represent Mattson at any time following the initial police lineup.

It is possible that Dingle was legitimately confused by Gubler's presence at the lineup. Gubler did not speak to Mattson one-on-one, as he was there only as part of his duties as a public defender. In fact, Gubler himself did not even know if his office had been appointed to represent this particular suspect. As events would later unfold, it was determined that Gubler had never been appointed by his office to represent Mattson or any of the participants in the lineup. From Dingle's perspective, Mattson had not been assigned counsel, and as a result, he was compelled to inform the suspect of his rights prior to any discussion with him, even though Mattson was the one who had initiated the exchange.

In the early afternoon, Mattson made his first appearance before a magistrate of the North Las Vegas Criminal Court to be arraigned. He was advised of his arrest charges by the judge, along with his right to counsel and his right to have counsel appointed for him by the state if he was unable to afford one.

Later that day, uncharacteristic of these circumstances, Dingle and Mattson continued their discussion regarding the North Las Vegas kidnapping and rape. Mattson talked openly about his part in this crime and also brought up a similar incident in Huntington Beach, California—the kidnapping of Kiz Livingston, although the victim was only identified by name later. This time, the interview lasted almost four hours and only began after Dingle again read Mattson his rights.

The following day, September 27, Dingle met with Mattson a third time, and Mattson openly confirmed his involvement in both cases and subsequently made a full confession to each allegation. The confession was tape-recorded, a transcript was prepared, and Mattson was given an opportunity to read and sign the typed transcript on each page. In doing so, Mattson was one step closer to being removed from society for the rest of his life.

THREE

CALIFORNIA

During the first week of October, Deputy Public Defender Rick Ahlswede was appointed to represent Mattson. Ahlswede was a former district attorney for Reno, Nevada, and as a district attorney, he was responsible for more death-penalty convictions than anyone else in the state. After his time as district attorney, Ahlswede switched tables in the courtroom, taking a position as a public defender in North Las Vegas.

Dingle, excited about having obtained a confession from Mattson, followed established protocols and advised Ahlswede of some developments in the California case as well as the potential for other unsolved crimes in which Mattson might be involved. From Dingle's perspective, his work on Mattson's case was beginning to look like an opportunity that usually takes a detective's career to the next level. Covering all the established legal guidelines, he also put Ahlswede on notice that Detective Branch had prepared a declaration for a criminal complaint against Mattson and, as a result, California issued a felony arrest warrant for him. Because of this, Ahlswede advised Mattson not to speak with Dingle anymore. However, after considering the severity of the charges filed against him, Mattson elected to waive his attorney-client privilege, and Ahlswede, after consulting with his client, subsequently granted Dingle permission to talk to Mattson again. Ahlswede would later say that although he knew Mattson was being investigated for crimes that he may have committed in California, he did not know his client was being investigated for murder. And so, Dingle continued to interview Mattson four or five times a week in the month of October, without feeling it necessary to inform Ahlswede every time.

In early November, Dingle was contacted by Detective Stuart Reed of the Los Angeles County Sheriff's Department, Homicide Division. Putting his previous discussions with Mattson aside, Dingle, based upon his years of experience in dealing with murderers, suspected that Mattson had been involved in one or two murders, but until the phone call from Reed, he was not aware of any actual ongoing homicide investigations in which Mattson might actually be implicated.

On November 7, Reed flew to North Las Vegas with the expectation of interviewing Mattson regarding his suspicions. Upon his arrival, he met with Dingle, and the two men tried unsuccessfully to contact Ahlswede to inform him of Reed's intention to interview Mattson.

The next day, never having heard back from Ahlswede, Dingle and Reed met with Mattson as planned to discuss the crimes he was accused of committing against Cheryl and Kiz. Reed, without Ahlswede's permission, proceeded with his trip's objective and questioned Mattson.

Reed started out their conversation by advising Mattson that he did have the right to have his attorney in the room during the interview. Mattson told Reed that he was willing to speak with him without Ahlswede's presence.

Reed, in his enthusiasm to solve his case, moved forward with the questioning of Mattson. With a tape recorder recording their conversation, Reed told Mattson that he was investigating a case involving a girl from the Santa Fe Springs area and asked Mattson if he knew anything about the crime. Matter-of-factly, Mattson told Reed that he knew the girl was dead. Trying to suppress his rising excitement, Reed informed Mattson that he and his Plymouth were identified by a custodian from Santa Fe High School. At this point, Mattson admitted that he had kidnapped and sexually assaulted Cheryl Gutierrez. Reed had Mattson's statement transcribed and given to Mattson for him to read and sign.

Even with the reminder of his right to remain silent and to have an attorney typed across the top of the page, Mattson signed the statement without hesitation.

He then volunteered, in his soft-spoken voice, "I will give you one you do not know about."

Mattson proceeded to meticulously describe the murder of another girl, gave detailed directions to the location of her body, and told Reed about a piece of paper in his car on which a map of the site would be found. This statement, too, was recorded, transcribed, and signed by Mattson.

"Michael, before I can search your car for that map you described, I will need your permission," Reed informed him.

"Okay. No problem," Mattson responded with a sheepish grin.

"Does that mean I *have* your permission?" Reed pressed.

Mattson formally gave Reed permission to search his car for the piece of paper, which would eventually lead detectives to Adele's body.

Mattson, feeling somewhat relaxed with Reed, stated that he may have committed additional crimes that he blocked from his memory. He suggested that drugs might help him recall more details of his crimes. Reed made it very clear that he was unable to assist Mattson with this request and suggested that, as an alternative, a psychiatrist might be able to help him. Mattson appeared to be more concerned with his ability to get drugs than his ability to get psychological or medical assistance. Mattson had started abusing reds, barbiturates, sleeping pills, speed, Methedrine, marijuana, LSD, and angel dust at the age of 16, and he continued to do so as an adult. Since his capture, none of these drugs had been available to him, so he was probably suffering through some type of physical and psychological withdrawal. It is possible that Mattson was simply trying to exchange information for drugs.

Reed would only promise that he would forward Mattson's concerns and need for drugs to the proper authorities, doctors, or whoever might be interested in helping Mattson with his addiction. Reed believed that Mattson found it easier to talk about the details of his crimes when he identified himself as a person who was drug-crazed and in need of help.

Reed, acting upon the detailed information supplied by Mattson and the map found in his abandoned Plymouth, contacted the California authorities and directed them to search for Adele's body in the area described by the suspect. Her remains were found exactly where Mattson indicated they would be.

The Hillside Strangler task force, also having seen Dingle's teletype, contacted Dingle for a meeting with

Mattson. Dingle once again became the facilitator for the meeting. His role was becoming routine. Every time an agency or another detective wanted to interrogate Mattson, Dingle found himself in the middle. Mattson enjoyed the attention, but one would speculate that so did Dingle. After all, he may have been responsible for catching a serial killer.

A two-man task force from Riverside, California, also traveled to North Las Vegas, wanting to talk to Mattson regarding their investigation of the kidnapping and murder of a 16-year-old girl from Hemet named Deanna Musquiz. Dingle once again sat in observation.

These investigators appear to be making headway with Mattson, Dingle thought to himself. In fact, the suspect began giving the two California detectives details never printed in any newspaper and unknown to the general public. However, as he did with every other investigator who questioned him, Mattson started to toy with them, giving them just enough information so they would remain interested and continue their conversation with him. In this instance, the younger of the two investigators became so frustrated with Mattson's game that, at one point, he grew aggressive in his attempt to obtain the information and confession they were trying to get. Mattson, who never liked aggressive behavior directed toward him, stopped talking. The interview was over, and the detectives left without the confession they had hoped to obtain.

After the meeting about Deanna's murder, Dingle decided to confront Mattson more directly about why he was so willing to speak with California law enforcement agencies. Dingle's curiosity was beginning to mount. Mattson's answer was simple, even somewhat logical. Mattson recognized that he was caught and "done" in Nevada. He had confessed to the kidnapping and rape of Sonia Lindsey, and he realized that he would have to go to prison. He explained to Dingle that the prison in Carson City, Nevada, where he would probably be sent, had been built in the 1880s and would not be a comfortable place to do his time. Therefore, if he had to do time in prison, he preferred that it be in California.

"Why California?" Dingle asked in a quizzical manner.

"Hell, are you kidding me?" Michael retorted. "The environment is better, and besides that, I would be able to work in the kitchen and have access to liver!"

Not being able to resist the obvious question, Dingle wondered why Mattson wanted liver. "This may sound like a dumb question, but what's the deal with liver?"

Mattson, with his usual sheepish grin, replied, "For masturbation."

Dingle could only shake his head. Mattson was clever, and Dingle had to give him credit. For a high school dropout, he was smarter than Dingle had first assumed from his actions with Sonia. He never blurted out any answers, and every answer he gave while being questioned was clear and well thought-out. Mattson even gave clues as to how he wanted each subsequent interview to go. Anything to avoid sitting in a cell every day with the same routine.

Their next meeting brought another major breakthrough. Mattson, sipping on his usual cup of heavily-sugared coffee, began to tell Dingle a story of a girl he had picked up hitchhiking by Laguna Beach on her way to work at a motel. He took her to a wooded area by Duarte, where she begged him not to hurt her. She even told Mattson that her father would give him money if he let her go. Unlike with Kiz, however,

Mattson ignored her pleas, and he told Dingle how he had "hardcore" sex with her then strangled her. Dingle asked him what he defined as "hardcore sex," to which Mattson merely smiled and stated it meant "sodomy."

Afterward, he went on to say, he was sitting near the body when she suddenly sat up and began making moaning noises that unnerved him. He thought he had already successfully killed her. She began making sounds as if she was trying to speak but could only utter unintelligible moans, probably because he had crushed her larynx when he had attempted to strangle her. She turned her head from side to side, very slowly, confusedly, as if attempting to determine where she was and what was happening. She was sitting in a shallow makeshift grave, and Mattson had partially covered her body with leaves, twigs, and branches. When she finally noticed Mattson, she began making louder noises and seemed to be in a state of utter panic. She frantically began wiping away the dirt and debris that clung to her sweaty skin.

Mattson stared straight ahead as he explained to Dingle that he had strangled the girl a second time until she stopped moving altogether. That time, she was truly dead. Mattson smiled a sinister smile. He actually seemed to be bragging that he had the toughness to carry out this act not once, but twice. Dingle got the impression that Mattson was trying to relive the experience by describing it to him. Dingle felt the bile rise in his throat as he recalled his previous feelings of disgust for Mattson. Mattson also told Dingle that he often went back to the girl's gravesite to visit and talk to her. The young girl he was describing was Adele Jean Corradini.

Subsequently, Dingle acknowledged that these types of conversations with Mattson continued for approximately six months. Mattson asked to be put under the influence of drugs so he could potentially remember other crimes he might have committed. Dingle, still hoping to obtain other confessions for unsolved murders in California, agreed to have Mattson taken to the North Las Vegas Hospital, a nearby medical facility. Dingle, by that point, was on a mission. At the medical facility, Mattson was administered Brevital, a quick-acting, intravenous anesthesia similar to Pentothal, otherwise known as truth serum. Dr. O'Gorman, a psychiatrist, supervised the session.

The results of the experiment were alarming, though not fruitful in revealing any other crimes. Under the influence of the drug, Mattson could not be asked detailed questions. "Yes" and "no" answers were the most typical responses. From this session, Dingle was able to determine that Mattson was responsible for approximately fifteen to twenty murders in total. To determine this range, Dingle used a simple numbers count when asking his questions. He asked Mattson, "Have you murdered at least five girls?"

"Yes," was the response Mattson gave him.

When Dingle reached the range of "fifteen to twenty" girls, Mattson responded, "I don't know."

During the first session, they did learn that Mattson felt great remorse for killing Adele, but for some strange reason, he experienced none over little Cheryl.

Earlier when he had been questioned about his emotional response to his crimes, Mattson explained, "After I am done, I've killed them." He also explained that he had a high interest in sodomy, feeling that there was no difference between that and regular heterosexual sex.

During the course of the multiple investigations that were occurring surrounding the crimes Mattson was suspected of committing in California, Mattson's California parole officer also contacted Dingle to discuss Mattson's role in the murders of Cheryl Gutierrez and Adele Corradini. Upon his return to California in early 1978, Mattson transferred his parole from Oregon to California and was reporting to his parole officer each month as required. Given Mattson's attitude about the legal system, he probably saw his monthly parole meetings as nothing more than a joke, especially since when he and the other parolees would meet with their parole officers in a local park, they would often spend some of their time there buying and selling drugs, right under the parole officers' eyes. According to Mattson, his activities were never picked up on by his parole officer, a Hispanic woman in her late fifties. Dingle would later reflect that she was "kind of a mother figure who was very concerned that Mattson had committed these crimes while on her watch." Dingle could offer her no consolation. The crimes Mattson committed probably did occur on her watch.

After the first session with the psychiatrist, Mattson was later able to convince Dingle that another session with

Dr. O'Gorman might help him remember even more specifics about his crimes. Accordingly, Dingle arranged another session with the doctor. The meeting took place in a small interview room at the jail. The topic of conversation focused on the Deanna Musquiz murder. Dingle, still seeking a confession to assist the California authorities as well as to boost his professional career, was determined to pursue this issue. All three individuals sat so close together that their knees were touching. Mattson, in response to Dr. O'Gorman's questions regarding the details of the Musquiz case, was very relaxed and almost in a hypnotic trance as he answered.

Then the psychiatrist asked the cornerstone question: "Did you murder Deanna Musquiz, Michael?"

Mattson hesitated. Both the detective and the doctor leaned forward, anticipating the answer. Dingle could feel himself shaking with excitement. He had been waiting to hear this answer since the Riverside detectives had failed to obtain it during their interrogation of Mattson.

Mattson leaned forward and asked, "Do you think I did it, Doctor?"

Perhaps trying not to influence Mattson's answer, O'Gorman replied, "No, Michael, I do not think you did it."

Mattson leaned back and simply smiled at Dingle. The detective looked at the doctor in amazement. At this point, the session was over and the opportunity was lost for good, for Mattson never discussed Deanna again.

However, the investigators had enough evidence against Mattson to be able to successfully bring charges against him. The only question was where Mattson was going to stand trial first.

John K. Van de Camp, the Los Angeles County District Attorney, wanted Mattson to atone for his crimes in California, but Nevada was first in line because Mattson was already in custody there.

Because Mattson confessed and subsequently pleaded guilty at his Nevada trial in January 1979, he was convicted of the kidnapping and rape of Sonia Lindsey. While the judge sentenced Mattson to time in prison, there was no guarantee that he would not eventually be released to rape and murder again, especially considering he had already been in prison in

Oregon and managed to get released on early parole because of his good behavior. For this reason, Van de Camp wanted to have Mattson extradited to California to face the pending allegations against him there.

In July, the Los Angeles District Attorney successfully petitioned the court to have Mattson transferred to California to answer to the victims, their families, society, and the criminal justice system. Once in California, Mattson was charged with the willful, deliberate, and premeditated first-degree murders of Cheryl Gutierrez and Adele Corradini; the rape or attempted rape, and lewd or lascivious conduct on a child under the age of 14; the rape of Adele; the kidnapping of Cheryl and Adele; and the infliction of great bodily harm on both. With respect to his crimes against Kiz Livingston, Mattson was charged with kidnapping, rape, sodomy, and oral copulation.

In December, Mattson was brought to trial in Norwalk, California. Throughout the process, Mattson's attorney, Larry S. Beyersdorf, filed several motions seeking to suppress all the statements, admissions, and confessions Mattson had previously made in connection with the crimes he was charged with, on the grounds that certain promises were made to induce him to confess, that the arresting officers knew he was represented by counsel but neither notified said counsel nor sought permission from counsel in the Nevada proceeding, and, after he asserted his right to counsel during questioning, Dingle and Reed should have refrained from interrogating him. Furthermore, Mattson sought to suppress "items found in his automobile," claiming his consent to Dingle for the search of his car was unlawful because it was not "free and voluntary" and was given after he asserted his right to counsel. Mattson's attorney argued that Mattson's statements were made in "submission to authority," and were tainted by the statements that had been illegally obtained. Beyersdorf also filed a motion to suppress any evidence presented by the prosecuting attorney, David Feldman, regarding Mattson's statements concerning the whereabouts of Adele's body.

Mattson's motions were denied by the court, and after the prosecution and defense both presented their cases, a jury of his peers easily found Mattson guilty of the alleged crimes.

In an effort to receive a lighter sentence for his crimes, Mattson provided several witnesses, including family members and doctors, who all testified that he had a history of abuse, sociopathic behavior, schizophrenia, and severe drug and alcohol abuse. The judge, however, was not swayed by Mattson's arguments, and sentenced him to death. Mattson was ordered to be incarcerated on San Quentin's Death Row, pending any and all appeals filed on his behalf.

FOUR

MICHAEL DEE MATTSON

Even the type of person who can so easily snuff out the lives of other human beings is still entitled to the full protections of the law. Furthermore, the question of why an individual such as Mattson would commit the types of crimes he was accused of eventually arises. Certainly kidnapping, raping, sodomizing, and murdering anyone, much less young girls, is not normal behavior. *Who is Mattson? What made him who he is? What made him commit the acts alleged?*

Michael Dee Mattson (aka Michael Dee Golyer), was born on July 23, 1953, in the state of Utah. According to statements by his mother, Jackie Mattson Golyer, a simple woman with limited formal education, Michael, even when he was still in her womb, was beaten during her pregnancy by her abusive husband, "Dee Mattson," who apparently drank excessively. She stated that until Mattson was 6 years old, his father resented him on a daily basis, openly classified him as a weakling, outwardly called him a "sissy," and felt that something was wrong with him. In 1959, when Michael was only 6, his parents divorced. Soon thereafter, his mother married James Red Golyer, Michael's stepfather, who also had a reputation for having been abusive toward Jackie. When interviewed by Dr. Vicary, a court-appointed psychiatrist, Mattson's mother made it very clear that the other children, William, Ronald, and Barbara, never had to endure the same mistreatment and consistent beatings that Michael did.

There are other disturbing facts regarding Mattson's childhood. Again at age 6, his mother and stepfather had to take him to a psychiatrist because he was unmanageable in school. They were contacted by school officials who reported that Michael was constantly hitting other children, was sticking them with pins, and overall just could not be controlled.

Arguably, he may have been responding to the type of inappropriate behavior that he was witnessing on a regular basis at home.

Unfortunately, his antics took on a more serious turn. Both Mattson and his parents confirmed that as a child, he routinely set fires; that he had ripped the heads off some pet pigeons owned by their next-door neighbor; and, that around the age of 12, he had taken a 5-year-old boy into an orange field in the neighborhood, beaten the child, made him eat a rotten orange and some dirt, stuck a stick or broomstick up the child's rectum, and then made him walk home in the nude. Clearly by that time he was already out of control and on a path of destruction.

As he grew older, Mattson became more agitated. His mother and stepfather began to notice, among other things, that he would stare into space for extended periods of time. Sometimes, they noted, he would play the same song on the jukebox over and over again, would erupt in fits of anger for no apparent reason, and would take long walks into the desert by himself. These actions bewildered them.

It was also later revealed that between the ages of 12 and 16, Mattson had started taking drugs that included barbiturates, sleeping pills, marijuana, and LSD. Additionally, he drank hard liquor and beer frequently.

At 17, Mattson entered the army and was stationed in Oregon, where he subsequently went AWOL and committed his first major crime. The pieces to the puzzle of his own self-destruction were moving closer into place, and nothing, including the support of his loved ones, could stop it. Finally, in the summer of 1978, Mattson's inner struggle exploded. For approximately four months, his anger and violence became uncontrollable until he was finally caught and brought to justice in Nevada.

———◈———

It is easy for people to speculate as to why people do the things that they do. Good or bad, it does not matter. However, when an individual commits crimes like those committed by Mattson, the court goes through a process to determine whether or not the defendant has the mental fitness to stand trial. Such was the case with Mattson. Dr. Alfred Cooley, a court-appointed psychiatrist licensed to practice medicine in the state of California, interviewed Mattson in September 1979 to determine if he was mentally fit to stand trial.

Dr. Cooley began by asking Mattson about the types of drugs and alcohol he was using a year earlier when he committed the alleged crimes. Mattson admitted that for years he had been a heavy drinker and had also used PCP, or angel dust, repetitively. He also stated that he had taken "downers," sedative drugs like Seconal and Nembutal, for a long time. Dr. Cooley quickly determined that the use of all these drugs had contributed to disturbing Mattson's mental functioning for the majority of his youth and young adulthood.

Furthermore, Dr. Cooley felt that the use of these drugs and Mattson's "fragile ego structure" had combined to cause a breakdown of the usual ego functions. For Mattson, this meant psychotic thinking and behavior patterns.

Mattson's violent childhood seemed to have a direct impact on his adult behavior. According to Cooley,

Mattson had demonstrated a regressive pattern of sadistic action, with repetitive episodes determined by unconscious factors within him. Basically, Mattson repeatedly hurting his victims stemmed from unconscious behaviors attributed to his earlier years. His abuse of alcohol and drugs was probably the catalyst that caused a manifestation of those inner feelings. As an example, Mattson said that at the time he killed Cheryl, he was taking alcohol and PCP. In relation to Adele, Cooley believed that these same factors had operated to diminish Mattson's capacity to premeditate and deliberate in her death. If Cooley was correct and Mattson's behavior was the result of a mental defect, he would not have had the state of mind required to form the specific intent to commit the crimes. He simply acted.

Dr. Cooley formed the opinion that Mattson's judgment was impaired and had been so all his life. Furthermore, he considered Mattson a highly impulsive person. He also emphasized that Mattson's behavior patterns were driven by his inner conflicts, which had been present since childhood and manifested themselves in an aggressive manner because of the alcohol and drug use.

One of the major inner conflicts mentioned concerned Mattson's sexuality. In Dr. Cooley's opinion, Mattson had never made a definitive sexual maturation in either a homosexual or heterosexual direction. Supporting this opinion was Mattson's struggle with transvestitism, which indicated he was not sure whether he was a man, woman, or child. This distorted version of sexuality also led Mattson to have a confused picture of adult, male-female, consensual intercourse. Adding to his distorted point of view were two bad experiences he had while serving his prison term in Oregon. Mattson was apparently raped twice by two fellow convicts, and as a result, refused to leave his jail cell. These distortions also may have been the direct result of Mattson's drug and alcohol abuse. In fact, he had previously stated that he had dropped lysergic acid about twenty to thirty times, had been using PCP several times per week since 1975, and, on an average, consumed a case and a half of beer per day, which would, beyond any doubts, have categorized him as an alcoholic.

Mattson existed in a disorientated state of mind. He often related very strange sexual forms of behavior, such as running around in fields nude and at times with women's clothes on, and repeatedly having intercourse with horses. In fact, as he recounted to Dr. Cooley, he preferred to have intercourse with horses instead of human beings. According to Dr. Cooley's psychiatric analysis, the horse, in the unconscious, represents an adult figure, a *big* adult figure, when one is a very small child. The horse is selected because the individual is reproducing his or her own experiences or fantasies as a child.

Relating Mattson's background to the crimes committed, Cooley hypothesized that when Mattson strangled his victims, he may have been unconsciously trying to strangle his mother to get even with her for failing to protect him from all the beatings he took as a young child and teenager.

Maria Jacobs was a counselor for Family Services of Long Beach. She held a bachelor's degree in science and had spent four years in medical school at the University of Mexico City. As a condition of Mattson's Oregon parole and subsequent relocation back to California, she met with him and his mother for a total of sixty hours.

According to Jacobs, she also met with Mattson's mother alone without Michael's knowledge. His mother told Jacobs that her underwear and makeup disappeared regularly, and that Michael would lock himself in the bathroom for hours and nobody would know what he was doing. She also stated that she was concerned about him because she was afraid he was using her clothes. She confirmed that on at least one occasion, when Mattson was a teenager or in his early twenties, she'd found him in a field dressed as a girl dancing for a group of children.

A short time after their meeting, Jacobs received a telephone call from Mattson's mother, who was upset because Michael had been crying for four days in a row and was unable to stop. His mother explained that he and a group of his peers had been using drugs. The next day, Mattson went to see Jacobs and told her that he had been smoking angel dust with some friends and they had all "freaked out."

Sometime later, Jacobs would comment that when she interviewed Mattson, he always appeared to be out of touch with reality; his voice was always monotonous, difficult to hear, and very low. Furthermore, she noted that he'd talk to himself, and that his eyes always expressed a look of profound danger and hatred and would harden at the least touch of emotion. Following another visit with Mattson and his mother, Jacobs made the following entry into her records:

> Michael came with his mother. As the time passes by he seems to show more psychotic symptoms. He shows no concern, no remorse, no desire to live with society. He claims he doesn't understand what anyone says, even a simple telephone conversation. He says he only talks to himself, and when he is with somebody, he fantasizes so he does not have to listen because he does not understand anybody.

She also noted that Mattson had a very low opinion of women. To him, women were whores who needed to have the "shit" beaten out of them. It would later be determined through a psychiatric evaluation that he was "jealous of women because they got to wear pretty things." Jacobs associated this attitude with Mattson's relationship with his mother. In a second journal entry, Jacobs noted:

> Behind all the incidents, his mother appears to be the one woman he can get even with. He knows

how to hurt her and she, no doubt, appears afraid of him. He has a low, poor, dirty opinion about women. In a very ambivalent conversation he uses contradictory and cynical statements. I do feel he could kill women because of his hatred.

In another entry she added:

I see Mike potentially dangerous, not able to face every day life. He has no goals, no plans for his future. He is not in touch with his feelings and he is not in touch with reality. He has not adjusted in any way to the community. He is not responsible for his own behavior and has expressed an interest in wanting to return to prison after having been in a quarrel with his family over his not wanting to work.

Jacobs' last meeting with Mattson was approximately twelve months before he killed his first known victim—Cheryl Gutierrez.

In July 1979, Mattson was moved to California to stand trial. Dr. William Vicary was appointed by the court to examine the defendant. Vicary had completed his undergraduate work at the University of New

Mexico and spent three years at Harvard Law School, where he graduated with a juris doctorate. From there, he went to the University of Southern California medical school, received an MD, and subsequently spent three years in residency at USC Medical Center in Los Angeles.

Initially, Vicary formed the opinion that Mattson's mental capacity at the time he committed the crimes was probably not substantially impaired, and therefore he did not qualify to be excused from responsibility.

However, after further interviewing Mattson, Dr. Vicary's opinion changed, and he reached a contradictory conclusion that Mattson had indeed been suffering from a major mental illness since the age of 17. He determined that Mattson was living in another world. "He is just crazy. His thinking is delusional at times and, at best, it is illogical and irrational," Vicary noted.

When pressed by the prosecution, Vicary disclosed that in his professional opinion, Mattson had been suffering from psychosis, which is a mental impairment to such an extent that one's cognition, perception, mood, memory, and other mental abilities are impaired from properly assessing reality. He also felt that Mattson may have been suffering from chronic schizophrenia, which causes a split between what a person is saying and his or her emotional response. For example, someone with chronic schizophrenia can be talking about a very tragic event and be smiling.

Vicary further noted that Mattson had a long history since childhood of doing illegal antisocial activities, and had expressed sentiments that he didn't care what other people thought or felt. He also expressed that he believed in Satan, which Vicary found strange because Mattson, a professed atheist with no belief in God, bore a tattoo of a crucifix on his right arm. All these scenarios are contradictory and represent just another sign that Mattson was a confused individual.

In addition, Mattson told the doctor that he wished he were a woman, that if he could have a sex-change operation he would have one, and that once completed, he would become a whore. He told Dr. Vicary that he hated women and when asked why, he replied, as previously mentioned, that he was jealous of them because they got to wear pretty things.

Despite all the professional psychological opinions, the Court determined that Mattson was competent to stand trial and also held that he was legally sane for the purpose being able to be sentenced to death. Yet whether anyone believes he was insane or simply misguided in his youth is of little consequence. Young girls were kidnapped, raped, sodomized, brutally beaten, and murdered.

Finally, Mattson did explain why he'd killed his victims. He blamed his confinement and incarceration in the Oregon State Penitentiary on Jeanette Kors's testimony in court. Thereafter, he had decided to kill all his future victims to prevent them from being able to testify against him later. With such obviously strong feelings, it was surprising that he had let Kiz live. But then again, he probably would have killed her if he had found that big rock to bash in her head. This attitude, as well as his behavior, was against every principle that I had learned in my own childhood.

FIVE

MY BACKGROUND

Mattson's background could not have been more different from mine. I was delivered into this world by the hands of a midwife. The year was 1951, and we lived in the backwoods of Halifax, Virginia. It was a very small cabin that housed my grandparents, my older brother Charles, and my mother, Aretha, or "Cookie" as she was affectionately called. My father, Charlie, was in New York working and anxiously awaiting my arrival. It was a happy occasion, but six months after I was born, my mother died unexpectedly from spinal meningitis. She was only 22 years old. My father was devastated, but my brother and I were too young to feel the direct impact of such a loss. My stepmother, Elizabeth, and my stepbrother, Ted, entered my life a year or so later. Elizabeth raised Charles and me as if we were her own children. Her sense of Christian values, her attitude toward education, and her staunch position that all her sons would know, and practice, the social graces promulgated by the Amy Vanderbilts of the world molded me into the person I am today. She was a disciplinarian when she had to be, but mostly she was the kind and gentle mother every child should have.

As a family we lived for a number of years in Brooklyn, New York, and then, to the surprise of my brothers and me, my sister Lydia was born. She was ten years younger than me. My reign as the baby of the family was over. My younger brother Ralph came along three years later, and four female cousins came to live with us after both my father's sisters passed away. Needing more room and a nicer environment to raise a large family, my parents moved us to the Catskill Mountains in upstate New York. It was a small, rural, farming community that boasted only four hundred or so inhabitants, including the cats and dogs. We only had a part-time constable to keep the peace, which wasn't so difficult because everyone knew each other. It was a fabulous place to grow up and consistent with my mother's desire to establish us on a social level.

My father—who made his living driving tractor trailers—insisted that when I took on a part-time job, half of my earnings, which I earned through tips, went to the household. At 14, I had two paper routes. I delivered the morning paper before school at 5:30 a.m. and the evening paper after I got home from school at 4:00 p.m. My father had a firm belief that the men of the household had the responsibility to take care of the homestead. He developed this value after his own father abandoned him, his mother, and his two younger sisters. He can still vividly remember how he saw my grandmother weep when she and her three children returned home one day and found everything in their home gone, with the exception of one mattress on the floor and a pot of grits on the stove. Eventually, he had to quit high school and work to help support the family.

Dad had an added old-fashioned expectation that as men, we had an obligation to watch after the women in our family, and each other as well. Before moving upstate, when I was about 7, my brothers and I were playing in the local fenced-in park across the street from our house. A much older boy walked up to my brother Ted and broke an egg over his head. As we walked home with the egg yolk dripping down Ted's face, we knew our father would handle the situation. He was truck-driver tough. When we arrived home, we showed our father what had happened. He only had one question—he wanted to know what we had done about it. When we responded that we had done nothing, and that we had come home to show him what had happened, he took off his belt, chased us back across the street, and ordered us not to come home until we found the kid who had hit our brother with the egg. We found him, decided he was much smaller than that belt-wielding truck driver at home, and took care of business. We never forgot the lesson, and on more than one occasion, others learned that it was not advantageous to take on any one of us. I had a wilder side than the rest of my brothers and never took the time to reason out anything. If someone attempted to harm anyone in my family, I was the one who stepped up and straightened the person out. That was the way it was for years, until we grew into young adults and began to move in different directions.

We attended private schools and were raised in the Catholic faith. As an altar boy, I served mass every Sunday and never missed a Holy Day of Obligation.

I was also active with the Boy Scouts of America. I enjoyed the experience and became an Eagle Scout. The basic philosophy of scouting is duty to God and country, obeying the law, helping other people, and being morally straight. I walked the walk and I talked the talk. All the principles that I learned from my parents, scouting, church, and school were instilled in me when I left for Howard University in September 1970.

Still living somewhat on the wild side, it took me seven years to graduate from college. During that time, my parents separated and eventually divorced. I was greatly upset by it, but my sister Lydia was the one who suffered the ultimate impact. On one of my rare visits back home, I found my sister and brother being cared for by a housekeeper. My mother was away on a temporary assignment for her job in New York City. While I was eating dinner one night, a man in his early twenties came to the front door. I had never seen him before, but he told me he was there to see Lydia, who was only 13 years old at the time. Lydia explained to me that he was a friend of the housekeeper whom she had met earlier, but I refused to let him in the house, and he left, only to try to see Lydia again the next evening.

I had a long talk with Lydia and the housekeeper, and told them that it made no sense for that much older individual to be coming around to visit with Lydia. The housekeeper thought I was overreacting and didn't perceive the person as a threat. I called my mother in New York City and told her about the situation. She was unaware of it before I called, but assured me that she would be home soon and told me not to worry about it.

I returned to college, putting the events behind me. Within six months, though, I learned that the same man had violently raped Lydia on one of his return visits. My family kept the news from me just as Lydia had kept the matter secret herself until she was past any reasonable time to have her pregnancy ended safely. The matter was kept entirely within the family. No criminal charges were ever filed, and the man was never formally punished.

This sent me over the edge of reason. I blamed myself for the attack because I had a bad feeling about the man, although I did nothing to stop him from hurting my baby sister. I packed a suitcase, loaded my gun, and headed back home. Having heard the rapist was still in the area and living in the next town over, I searched for him for the better part of a week, but the word that I was looking for him got out and he went into hiding until my mother and sister finally convinced me to return to campus. Over the next year, I made occasional visits home, and every time I returned home, he would disappear. Eventually, I was told—falsely, I discovered years later—that he was dead, and I stopped my quest for vigilante revenge. If I had ever found him, I know I would have killed him for what he did to my sister.

Coincidently, during part of the time I was attempting to find this man, Mattson was engaged in his own crime spree. Of course I didn't know then that our lives would cross when his rampage was over and his right to counsel would bring him into my life. The role I was to play in his life would challenge the principles I had held dear since childhood and rekindle my feelings toward the circumstances surrounding my sister.

SIX

MY DILEMMA

In July 1982, my summer was interrupted by a telephone call from Ron Smith, one of my former law school professors. Ron and I had become acquainted during my first year of law school. He had been my instructor for Torts and we grew close throughout the year. After he returned my first law school exam with a failing grade, he took me under his wing, mentoring me throughout that first scary year. During the process, we had become friends. He and his wife Jennifer were constant dinner companions with my wife Betty and me when there was a break in my studies. Ron also gave me opportunities from time to time to work on special projects with him. He was engaged in an active law practice throughout my law school years, specializing in civil litigation and criminal law defense.

Over the phone, Ron spoke in a very excited tone: "Jim, still have an interest in criminal law?"

"Of course," I replied casually. I didn't know where his question might be leading.

"I just found out today that I was appointed by the California Supreme Court to represent some guy on death row, and I want to know if you'd be interested in assisting me with the case."

"Hell yeah, I'm interested. What's it all about?" I rose to my feet. "What did he do?"

"I don't have all of the details yet, but if he's on death row, he's obviously been convicted of murder."

"Well, whatever. I'm in." I was elated to have this opportunity handed to me.

Ron knew I enjoyed criminal law, with all of its mystery and intrigue. Plus, I would get the opportunity to work shoulder-to-shoulder with him, a former district attorney with Riverside County who had a vast amount of experience that I could soak up. As I thought about the opportunity that had just been given to me, my thoughts were interrupted by Betty.

"Who was that?" she asked, sitting down in the recliner across from me. She could clearly see my excitement.

"That was Ron," I exclaimed. "He wants *me* to assist him with a death penalty appeal to the *California Supreme Court*!"

"Really? What's it all about?" She leaned forward, excited for me.

"Well, I really don't know. He didn't have any details. He just asked me if I'd help him out, and I said I would. It doesn't matter what the case is."

"Sure it does," Betty countered. "Whatever the person did, the crime *had* to involve someone getting *killed*! Even I know that."

"I guess," I responded. "Let's just wait and see when I get the package from Ron."

Several days later, I received my copies of the four thousand pages of transcripts and exhibits from Mattson's original trial in 1979. My mouth dropped when I opened my front door to see two large, heavy boxes being delivered by the UPS driver. Having reviewed other trial transcripts for research, I expected a large envelope at best. As I perused binder after binder of text and exhibits, I began to wonder what I had gotten myself into. I was in for some serious reading.

The first order of business was to review the precise charges filed against Mattson that had ultimately led to his conviction. The next step was to review the complete facts, transcripts, and exhibits, sifting out key points and issues. The third and final step was to apply the facts to the legal principles and determine if there had been any violations of Mattson's rights that could become the basis for a successful appeal.

Ron's directive was clear and to the point—our job was to get the inmate off death row, or get his conviction overturned altogether. I began reading through the material in the early afternoon, each page taking on a life of its own and forcing me to look into the depths of my own soul. This man, young as he was, was a sexual predator of the worst kind. How could our objective be to set him free? My contempt for him was growing with every page I turned. I could feel myself becoming enraged that such a person could even be alive.

I skipped ahead when I realized that one victim, Kiz Rene Livingston, had survived the ordeal and testified against Mattson. The transcripts contained sixty-four pages of gut-wrenching testimony by Kiz who, on several occasions, could only nod to questions being asked because she was too emotionally choked up to speak. The judge, moved by compassion, called more than one recess to give Kiz an opportunity to compose herself. This young, innocent girl was being forced to relive every dreadful moment with her assailant staring at her from across the room.

As I read the transcript I could only imagine her horror. My thoughts constantly drifted back and forth between Kiz and my sister Lydia. It was becoming difficult to distinguish between the two in my mind.

———◦◦———

On July 10, 1979, the Los Angeles County District Attorney's Office filed thirteen criminal counts against Michael Dee Mattson. They included such charges as rape, the intent to commit serious bodily injury, lewd and lascivious acts, sodomy, kidnapping, robbery, and murder.

On July 25, 1979, Mattson was arraigned, and unlike in his Nevada trial, he entered a plea of not guilty to all thirteen counts.

On October 30, 1979, Judge William E. McGinley appointed Dr. George Y. Abe and Dr. Seymour Pollak to conduct a psychological examination of Mattson and determine his mental fitness to stand trial. Both doctors were required to submit reports of their findings to the court. During this same time frame, Mattson, through his attorney Larry S. Beyersdorf, the public defender assigned to represent him, entered an additional plea of not guilty by reason of insanity.

On February 15, 1980, a jury of twelve of Mattson's peers were impaneled and sworn in to hear the case. Six men and six women were selected by the attorneys to sit on Mattson's jury. Mr. John Hardee was elected to be the jury foreman by the rest of the jurors.

David Feldman, the district attorney assigned to prosecute Mattson, questioned Kiz on February 19, 1980, about what happened after she became aware that Mattson was driving in the wrong direction once she got into his vehicle.

FELDMAN: Did you say anything at that time or indicate that you wanted to go some other way?

KIZ: Well, I think I went into shock or something, because I saw a knife in his hand.

FELDMAN: When you saw the knife in his hand, what if anything occurred after that?

KIZ: He told me to lock the door.

FELDMAN: Now when you saw the knife in his hand, where was it, how was it held, and where was it at?

KIZ: God, it was just real close to me. I think by my leg.

FELDMAN: He had a knife, he was driving, so the hand closer to you was the right hand?

KIZ: Yes.

FELDMAN: Was that the hand the knife was in, or the left hand, the side furthest away from you?

KIZ: The right hand.

FELDMAN: When you say close to you, what part of you?

KIZ: By my leg, by my side. I am not sure.

FELDMAN: By your thigh or your side?

Kiz moved her head up and down without saying anything.

FELDMAN: You have to speak up.

KIZ: Yes.

FELDMAN: Now when you looked down and saw that knife, was he just holding it?

KIZ: He was putting it by me, told me not to make any motions or anything like that, so people would not know something was wrong.

FELDMAN: After you saw the knife were you struck?

KIZ: Yes.

FELDMAN: How many times were you struck?

KIZ: It was a few. I can't remember the exact number.

FELDMAN: Where were you struck?

KIZ: On the face.

FELDMAN: With what?

KIZ: His hand. He backhanded me.

FELDMAN: Did he say anything?

KIZ: Well, I was crying and he was telling me to stop.

FELDMAN: Did you continue to cry?

KIZ: Yes.

FELDMAN: Then he struck you?

KIZ: Yes. He just kept yelling at me and telling me not to try and make anybody suspicious.

FELDMAN: Did you stop crying or continue to cry?

KIZ: I was crying all the time.

FELDMAN: Did he say he would do anything…?

KIZ: He told me he would kill me if I didn't shut up.

Mattson continued driving and screaming at Kiz until they reached a secluded wooded area off the 605 Freeway in the Los Angeles area.

KIZ: He reached over and opened my side of the door and started pushing me out.

FELDMAN: Did you get out?

KIZ: He pushed me out of the car.

Kiz, terrified, found herself in an out-of-the way place that had a "bunch of mud ditches and trees around."

FELDMAN: When he stopped, did he say anything to you about your clothing?

KIZ: He told me…to take off my pants.

FELDMAN: Did you do it the first time he told you to do it?

KIZ: No. I was hesitating, and he started pulling them.

FELDMAN: Did he ever strike you?

KIZ: Yes.

FELDMAN: Where did he strike you?

KIZ: In the face.

FELDMAN: Were those pants taken off?

KIZ: Yes.

FELDMAN: Completely off?

KIZ: They were off.

FELDMAN: Where you wearing underpants?

KIZ: He took those off too.

FELDMAN: Did he give you any other instructions?

KIZ: He just pulled down his own pants.

FELDMAN: Did he give you any instructions?

KIZ: He told me to suck him.

Kiz then described in detail what she was forced to do. She said that she didn't fight back only because she was afraid of Mattson and didn't want to get hurt.

FELDMAN: What happened next?

KIZ: I don't know how to say it.

FELDMAN: What did he do?

KIZ: He put his penis inside me.

Kiz told how Mattson continued to violate her young body "for awhile." She continued to weep on the stand as she described how "rough" Mattson was while he raped her.

FELDMAN: What happened after that?

KIZ: He told me to bend over.

FELDMAN: And did you?

KIZ: I didn't want to. I was trying to fight him.

FELDMAN: And then what happened?

KIZ: And he just told me if I didn't do it he was going to kill me.

FELDMAN: Did you bend over then?

KIZ: Yes.

FELDMAN: What happened after you bent over?

Kiz began to graphically describe how Mattson sodomized her. On the stand, Kiz became more emotional as she described his rough behavior and her extreme amount of pain. Her tearful pleas for Mattson to end the assault went without notice as he continued for longer than she cared to remember.

FELDMAN: What did he do next?

KIZ: He sat on my back.

FELDMAN: While you were down on the ground?

KIZ: Yes.

FELDMAN: And then what happened next?

KIZ: He started playing with my hair and he took off his belt.

FELDMAN: What did he do with that belt?

KIZ: He was playing with my hair and he told me he was going to hang me from that tree.

FELDMAN: What did you say or do?

KIZ: I was just crying, you know, and saying, "Oh God, please let me live."

Kiz paused for a moment to compose herself on the stand, and then continued.

KIZ: And then he just sat there for a few minutes playing with my hair. And finally he threw the belt and he just said, "I can't kill you."

FELDMAN: Then did he tell you to put your clothes back on?

KIZ: He didn't let me for a few minutes. Then he just kept saying, "You have got a lot of faith in that guy up there, don't you?"

Kiz was unable to continue testifying, and a recess was taken to give her time to compose herself.

When Kiz was able to continue, she concluded her testimony with a detailed account of Mattson dropping her off at her girlfriend's home where she immediately took a shower before calling the police.

When I finished reading this part of the transcript, I sat back in my chair and closed my eyes for a moment to think about what I'd just read. My concentration was broken by Betty.

"How late are you going to be up?" she asked.

I looked up and saw her standing there in her robe and slippers, and realized that the entire day was already gone.

Betty could obviously see by my wrinkled brow that I was extremely upset about something. Over the next thirty minutes, Betty could only stare and listen in increasing disbelief as I gave her an overview of the crimes Mattson had been convicted of committing.

When I finished, her only comment was, "For God's sake, Jimi. He's right where he belongs, on *death row*!"

Over the next several days, I reviewed the rest of the original trial transcript.

Throughout the trial, the prosecution, led by Feldman, called a number of witnesses, including Sylvia Gutierrez and Esther Gutierrez, Cheryl's sister and mother, who both offered testimony as to the circumstances surrounding the events that led to Cheryl's disappearance that fateful day.

> **FELDMAN:** Now Sylvia, directing your attention to the 14th of July of 1978, do you remember that day?

> **SYLVIA GUTIERREZ:** Yes.

> **FELDMAN:** Did you go somewhere that day?

> **GUTIERREZ:** Yes.

> **FELDMAN:** Where to?

> **GUTIERREZ:** To the swimming pool.

> **FELDMAN:** Keep your voice up, please, and the swimming pool is where?

> **GUTIERREZ:** In Santa Fe Springs.

> **FELDMAN:** And is the school at Santa Fe Springs?

GUTIERREZ: Yes.

FELDMAN: What school is that?

GUTIERREZ: Santa Fe High.

FELDMAN: And at Santa Fe High was there a swimming pool?

GUTIERREZ: Yes.

FELDMAN: And who went with you to that swimming pool?

GUTIERREZ: My little sister and my other little sister.

FELDMAN: Two sisters? What were their names?

GUTIERREZ: Toni and Cheryl.

FELDMAN: And how old was Toni?

GUTIERREZ: Five.

FELDMAN: And Cheryl?

GUTIERREZ: Nine.

FELDMAN: Nine? How old were you then?

GUTIERREZ: Eleven.

FELDMAN: And who took you there?

GUTIERREZ: My mother.

FELDMAN: Did she drive you there?

GUTIERREZ: Yes.

The next series of questions and answers focused on Sylvia and Cheryl disagreeing on whether or not to stay at the pool. Sylvia had told Cheryl to go and call their mother at the pay phone in the building by the pool. Cheryl, according to Sylvia, became upset, sat down in a hallway by the pool area, and refused to make the call. Sylvia, at this point in the testimony, became choked up and could only nod or shake her head in response to the questions being asked. Gaining her composure, she continued to answer the questions gently posed by Feldman.

FELDMAN: Did you call your mom?

GUTIERREZ: No. No. Because they wouldn't let me use the phone.

FELDMAN: What happened then?

GUTIERREZ: So I was looking for Cheryl, so I went—

FELDMAN: Just let's take it easy. You went to use the phone, and you last saw Cheryl sitting down in the hall, right?

Becoming upset, Sylvia could only nod her head up and down.

FELDMAN: When you went to use the phone, they told you that you couldn't use it?

Still upset, Sylvia once again could only shake her head up and down.

FELDMAN: Did you go back where you left Cheryl?

Sylvia responded by nodding her head, and Feldman instructed her that she would have to give verbal answers. Young Sylvia did her best to answer the questions while fighting back her tears. She explained how she began looking for her younger sister because she had disappeared. She searched and searched in a frantic manner until her mother arrived at 5:00 p.m. to pick them up.

Feldman's last question said it all.

FELDMAN: Did you ever see your sister alive again?

Breaking down for the final time, little Sylvia shook her head from side to side and finally composed herself enough to choke out the answer that will probably haunt her forever.

GUTIERREZ: No.

Esther Gutierrez, Cheryl's mother, took the stand right after Sylvia. Over the next hour, she testified to what happened after her arrival at the pool. Her frantic search for her missing child netted negative results. Cheryl was gone. Recognizing the gravity of the situation, she recalled calling her husband and the police soon thereafter.

Feldman went on to question Esther regarding the clothing Cheryl had worn to the pool that day, a bikini-styled bathing suit with a floral print—the same article of clothing that would later be used to determine that the limp body found at Whittier Narrows Recreation Area was that of her daughter.

A final question by Feldman ended Esther's grief-stricken testimony.

> **FELDMAN:** In July she was three or four months shy of her tenth birthday?

Putting her hands to her face to shield the tears, Esther fought to give the one-word response that was required.

> **ESTHER GUTIERREZ:** Yes.

Then, later in the trial, there was the testimony of Jo-Ann Corradini, who fought back her own tears as she explained how her daughter Adele left home that day heading for her job and the subsequent telephone call that alerted her to the fact that her daughter had never arrived at her place of employment at Dana Point.

After a series of basic background-type questions, Feldman delivered question after question regarding the morning Adele got up and dressed for work.

Jo-Ann told Adele to wear her favorite sweater because of the weather.

> **FELDMAN:** Was that the same one she wore when you last saw your daughter on the morning of the 6th of September?

> **CORRADINI:** Yes. [Choking back her grief] I told her, "Go in and put your sweater on." It was raining that morning and I distinctly told her to put that one on. That's why I remember!

The issue of the sweater was important. The sweater, along with the puka-shell necklace, was used as evidence that it was the body of Adele that had been found in a small makeshift grave that was discovered based upon a map drawn by Mattson. Mattson never even knew her name when he killed her.

On February 28, 1980, after thirteen days of testimony, the matter was submitted to the jury for consideration. They deliberated for three days, and on March 3, 1980, they brought back a verdict of guilty on twelve of the thirteen counts.

Well, there it was! Mattson had been found guilty of each count, with the exception of count five. From the evidence submitted at the trial, the prosecution could not prove that Mattson had actually sodomized Cheryl. Although fecal matter was present on her buttocks and inner thighs, the only evidence presented that initially raised the issue was based upon Mattson's statements of the act he had committed. Later, he recanted as much as he could to reduce his possibilities of conviction.

Even though the trial was over, a sentence still had to be passed. The defense called Dr. William Vicary to discuss his psychological examination of Mattson before the trial.

BEYERSDORF: Dr. Vicary, were you appointed by the court to examine Michael Mattson?

VICARY: I was.

BEYERSDORF: You are not privately retained by the defense; is that correct?

After testifying to his professional background, Dr. Vicary acknowledged that he was provided with background reports that he carefully read before he interviewed Mattson.

BEYERSDORF: After reading the information that was provided to you, did you form a tentative opinion of Michael Mattson's capacity?

VICARY: I did.

BEYERSDORF: What was that?

VICARY: That his mental capacity at the time of the crimes was probably not substantially impaired.

BEYERSDORF: Did you form a tentative opinion as to whether he suffered from serious mental illness?

VICARY: I did.

BEYERSDORF: What was that?

VICARY: That he did not.

BEYERSDORF: Did you then interview Michael Mattson?

VICARY: I did.

BEYERSDORF: What was the approximate length of that interview?

VICARY: I think it was a little over three hours.

BEYERSDORF: Did you form a final opinion as to whether Michael Mattson was sane at the time the alleged offenses were committed?

VICARY: I did.

BEYERSDORF: What was your opinion?

VICARY: That at the time of the alleged offenses he was not insane, and did not qualify to be excused from responsibility for the crimes.

BEYERSDORF: After interviewing Michael Mattson, did your opinion change with regard to his mental illness or lack thereof?

VICARY: It did. Initially, during the first hour of my interview, it became a question in my mind as to whether I was not facing an individual who unexpectedly in terms of my prior review of all the materials was not suffering from a major mental illness. For the next two hours during the interview I proceeded to test the hypothesis, and my conclusion was that he was indeed suffering from a major mental illness.

BEYERSDORF: Can you tell us how you tested the hypothesis?

VICARY: About every thirty to forty-five minutes a jailer would come by and look into the interview room, just checking to make sure that everything was alright. I think there were two deputies that shared this, and both of them were relatively soft benign-looking people, and they would smile—or they seemed like they were supportive or friendly and yet the defendant would turn around and mutter something, and a look of intense hatred, antagonism would come over his face which was very frightening to me, and sometimes that is the one thing we—we note in our profession is that sometimes our reactions tell us something about the patient.

His intensity was so out of proportion that it frightened me.

BEYERSDORF: Anything else?

VICARY: Yes. He told me at the age of 19, he began to hear voices, specifically someone calling his name, and that initially he thought somebody was playing tricks on him.

Another thing—and this is probably far more important—is that throughout the three hours that I had with him, despite the fact that we went over in detail several of the brutal crimes, he had a rather bland, unchanging expression on his face.

I came to the conclusion that he is in another world. He is crazy. His thinking is delusional.

Both sides continued to ask Dr. Vicary questions regarding whether or not Mattson was mentally ill or insane when he committed the crimes. After each side finished their questioning, the judge allowed each attorney to make a closing argument on the issue of Mattson's insanity.

Feldman, on behalf of the People, went first. His closing argument lasted thirty-three minutes.

If it pleases the Court, counsel for the defense, ladies and gentleman of the jury.

You heard all of the evidence presented. The charge was the killing of two little girls, Cheryl Gutierrez, 8 or 9 years old, Adele Corradini, 16 years old, and the assault, rape, kidnapping of Kiz Livingston, 15 years old.

Now take a look at what the defendant said to the officers, both to Dingle and Reed. The question was, "Are you out?" He says, "I am always out looking for girls."

He also said, "I don't go out looking for them but if I see them and the opportunity is where I won't be caught I take advantage, and I kidnap, rape, and kill them."

He said after the Oregon conviction, "I will not leave any witnesses alive."

He said, "I don't leave any evidence behind."

What he says is that no little girl is safe on the streets if she comes in front of his vision, and there aren't a lot of people around.

Every little girl is fair game for him, for his lust, for his passion, and for his disposing of the witness so he can't be prosecuted.

Now we have a multitude of testimony from psychiatrists, commonly referred in the trade as head shrinks or shrinks. They are trying to tell you what he is thinking. Virtually, an impossibility.

This isn't a man with a total absence of memory. Remember that he tells each of the officers about certain crimes and lays out details.

As an example, in the matter of Deanna Musquiz, whose death he now denies having had any complicity with, he had previously given details that only the killer would know. How could he have known that she was on her back, legs spread apart, her pants and clothing removed, she had large breasts, and the path taken in and out from the body to the street, and the street to the body? He could not have known these details unless he was the killer.

And when you look at all the facts, the ligature around the neck, the rape, his explanation, he puts a knife to her neck and took her in and told her he would kill her, told her to undress. None of the clothing was torn on any of the girls. So this case fits with all of the others.

Kiz Livingston survived. He tells us in his own words he intended to kill her. He looked for a rock to kill her. He got his belt to strangle her. She pleaded and prayed to the Lord above.

Obviously the Lord heard her because he backed away. It wasn't that he didn't intend to kill her. Remember the testimony was that something affected him and he just couldn't go through with it.

Now don't get me wrong. Sure, he has mental problems, but his mental problems are not such that he does not know what is going on, that he is not able to control himself.

We are looking at what the penalty should be. You know they don't want the death sentence, they want life without the possibility of parole.

I ask you simply, what was given to little Cheryl Gutierrez? Life without parole? Did he give her a choice? Did he ask her? No.

Was she safeguarded by counsel? No.

Was she legally executed, according to law? No.

Now when he put his belt around her neck, and he was strangling her and pulling it tight, and he is kneeling on her, and that child—you can visualize she is trying to save her breath, trying to gulp for air. Her eyes bulging, her lungs are pounding, nothing, good-bye, Cheryl, she is dead.

We go back to Adele, almost the same thing. He sat on her back, choked her to death with a belt the same way, but he didn't fully do it so she recovered. Well, suppose you had been choked very severely, and you recovered consciousness. Your throat is burning, your lungs are burning, your eyes are bulging. He made sure she was dead. He redid it. He guaranteed that she was dead.

Did she get life without parole? No.

He deserves the penalty of death for both the Corradini and the Gutierrez killings. You can't execute him two times. I think once would be enough.

Beyersdorf answered Feldman's comments with his own closing argument, which lasted eighty-four minutes.

Ladies and Gentlemen, Mr. Feldman, in referring to the death penalty, said, "If not Mattson, who?"

Well, ladies and gentlemen, I would ask the reverse of that question: if not Kenneth Bianchi, the L.A. strangler who killed five women and maybe a lot more, why anybody?

That is the great problem with the death penalty. One of the great evils of the death penalty is that it is applied so unequally.

I can understand the frustration everyone feels. I don't think I have picked up a paper in the last month where I haven't read about a murder, a series of murders.

I think we are all caught up with that frustration. I feel it as much as anyone else.

We all ask, "What should we do?"

Justice Mosk of the California Supreme Court originally in 1973 voted the death penalty cruel and unusual punishment. He said he was against the death penalty. In a more recent decision he said he had come full circle.

He said he had voted against it but the people of California responded quickly and emphatically… to callously declare that whatever the trends else-where in the nation, and the world, society in our state does not deem the retributive extinction of a human life to be either cruel or unusual.

He said, "The day will come when all mankind will deem killing to be immoral, whether committed by one individual or many individuals organized into a state. Unfortunately, morality appears to be a waning rule of conduct today, almost an endangered species in this uneasy and tortured society of ours; a society in which sadism and violence are highly visible and often accepted commodities, a society in which guns are freely available and energy is scarce, a society in which reason is suspect and emotion is king."

Michael Mattson crossed the line, I would suggest, rather early in life. You have heard a great deal about that from doctors. Failures, deviant behavior, character disorders, and a major mental illness, I would suggest to you, led to the deaths of these two girls.

So ladies and gentleman, what I am saying is that it all just doesn't fit into that little box Mr. Feldman has.

There is a great deal more here than somebody who has just a personality disorder, just a no-good person, something a great deal more.

There is a very sick person here, and I think the significant question is—and I think the question that you ought to all be asking yourselves is—are you going to vote to send somebody to death if he is seriously mentally ill, if he is suffering from a major mental illness, is that an appropriate sentence if that is the fact.

But who among us can really walk in Michael Mattson's shoes, can really sit down and say, I understand what must have been going through his mind, I have put a foot partway in the shoe in which he walks.

I have difficulty doing that. I tried and I think any person probably does, unless they have been subjected to the things that Michael Mattson was probably subjected to.

The crimes themselves reflect a very serious mental illness, and I think you would expect the doctors to come up with the opinions that they came up with.

So, ladies and gentlemen, we have a right to protect ourselves, there is no question of that. In terms of Michael Mattson, society has given us more than one way to protect ourselves.

Mental illness and mental disease are the key factors in this case. Obviously if he is insane he is not guilty. But we have found he is sane. But if he is seriously mentally ill, I would suggest to you that killing him is inappropriate.

I would suggest to you that it is not right to kill somebody who is seriously mentally ill, and I would suggest that there is the gravest danger of error on your part, for error on the psychiatrics' part, in this type of a case.

Three hundred years from now I suspect that we are going to have a much better insight into why people like Michael Mattson commit the offenses they commit.

One of my favorite quotations is from Clarence Darrow in 1924 where he said, "Behind many murders is a cause that drove the human machine out of control, yet we send men to death after listening to words that half the people don't really understand or fully comprehend."

I would ask that you not kill Michael Mattson, not just for Michael Mattson, but for our society and for yourselves, because I think we can adequately protect ourselves against people like Michael Mattson with a sentence of life without the possibility of parole.

Two days later, on March 5, 1980, the jury determined that Michael Dee Mattson had been sane at the time of the commission of the offenses, and eight days after that, on March 13, 1980, the jury fixed his penalty at death.

The clerk read the jury's verdict to the court.

The defendant in this case has been found guilty of murder in the first degree in Count I and the charge that the murder was committed under all of the charged special circumstances has been especially found to be true. We, the jury in the above-entitled action, Count I, fix the penalty at death.

On April 10, 1980, Beyersdorf, on behalf of Mattson, made a motion for a new trial and an additional motion to reduce the sentence from death to life imprisonment without the possibility of parole. Both were denied by Judge McGinley. Mattson was officially sentenced to death.

———◉———

Several weeks later, having finished my review of the facts and issues, it was time for me to consider any and all plausible arguments that might assist Mattson in his appeal. I could see a number of smaller issues that I could mention in my report, but one issue stood out to me in particular—Mattson's constitutional right to counsel had possibly been violated.

I saw a pattern throughout Mattson's files that disturbed me. The relationship that had developed between Detective Dingle and Mattson was not normal. They seemed to have developed a working relationship and spent an inordinate amount of time together while Mattson was awaiting trial. Sure, Dingle would read Mattson his rights every time they spoke, but how many times can you read a person his rights and continue to engage in conversations that were designed to get him to tell you crucial information without his attorney ever being in the room?

If my theory was correct, Mattson's conviction could in fact be reversed, which meant he might eventually be a free man again. Time stood still. I wondered how Ron was progressing. Surely, as a former prosecutor, he would have found the same violations.

The crimes committed by this man were contrary to every moral principle I had ever learned. Forget morals for a second. I was a father, with a 4-year-old son and a wife who was pregnant again; this time, Betty might give birth to a daughter—one who might fall prey to someone just like Mattson. Of course, I didn't want to think about such a possibility, but I also couldn't help my thoughts. And it was obvious that Betty was thinking along the same lines. No responsible person would want a self-confessed serial murderer and rapist of young girls like Michael Dee Mattson any place but in prison. Betty was right.

Mattson was simply a cold, ruthless killer devoid of conscience. If released, he would engage in the same behavior again with no remorse; of this, I felt certain. My opinion of Mattson was also supported by facts in the files I had been poring through.

Dr. Vicary, a California court-appointed psychiatrist, had stated under oath that the "defendant would return to the same environment and lifestyle, and if he ever got out he would be just like he was before he was taken into custody." I asked myself over and over whether I could ever be part of such a process. I knew that Mattson was exactly where he should be. How had I put myself in a situation that ultimately could help this kind of sociopath? *No wonder society has such a dim view of the legal profession*, I thought, somewhat remorsefully.

At the dinner table that night, Betty and I spoke briefly about the trial. She was still unhappy that I had agreed to represent the case, and it showed in her expression and tone of voice.

"With all that he's done, why would you want to help him?" she asked candidly. "Jimi, we have one child and another on the way. How can you possibly even *consider* doing anything to help someone like that get out of jail? He preys on *children*, for God's sake!"

Unfortunately, by the end of the evening, I was no closer to resolving my dilemma.

Mattson *was* guilty. He'd confessed to the felonies, he had been identified by one of the victims in court, and several doctors had determined he'd been sane at the time of his crimes, knowing right from wrong. Even so, I had agreed to take on the role of his attorney, and I had an obligation to him since he was my client. More importantly, I also had to keep in mind that ultimately, Ron had asked me to assist him with this appeal, and I did not want to disappoint him.

I went to talk to Ron about my concerns with representing Mattson. Ron's perspective was simple. He had been appointed to represent Mattson, and the crimes he had committed were just that—crimes. The victims were victims, and not any different from other victims who had met similar fates at the hands of others. For Ron, it was mechanical. We had a job to do to the best of our abilities and being the professional that he was, he was going to get it done. *We* had to get it done because I was a part of the defense team and he was relying on me to assist him during this process.

Relying on me, I thought. It was true. There was a voluminous amount of reading and analysis of the material to be done. Ron had asked me to help him and I had given him my word that I would. My personal feelings were not a consideration when I agreed to work with him on this project. Sure, I found the subject matter repugnant with every page I read. Did I envision my sister's face every time I read each account? Of course. It was hard not to.

I continued to read the key facts over and over. It never got easier. Kidnapping, raping, sodomizing, and murdering young girls is a detestable series of acts to any sensible individual. In fact, Judge Kennard, one of the justices from the California Supreme Court who heard the appeal, commented, "[W]e do the very best we possibly can under the circumstances. And if we do not attempt to do that, it's just anarchy." These words sent a clear message to everyone assigned to the trial. Judge Kennard then declared that he'd experienced no joy in having to listen to what Mattson had done, nor did he believe that anyone present would enjoy hearing the details of these crimes, but it was his final comment that resonated: "The fact of the matter is, *that's our job.*"

My feelings of confusion were beginning to dissipate somewhat. If I, as Ron's law clerk, were charged with Mattson's representation, it was my professional responsibility to do the best job I could. *The victims' rights can no longer be my concern*, I told myself, and sighed deeply. *My only responsibility to Mattson is to be competent in my pursuit of his defense.*

It became my mantra to put all personal issues aside.

I decided to discuss my findings with Ron. If he thought my discoveries were legitimate, then obviously, the next step would be to investigate the issue I had discovered more deeply. If he disagreed with me, then I was off the hook.

SEVEN

PROFESSIONAL OBLIGATION

A few days later, Ron and I met to go over our mutual findings. Ron was very excited because he had discovered that the trial judge had read the wrong jury instructions. He felt that it was prejudicially improper for the judge to instruct the jury that the governor may in the future commute or modify a sentence of life imprisonment without the possibility of parole to a lesser sentence that might include the possibility of parole. Ron felt that because of this mistake, the California Supreme Court would have to reduce Mattson's sentence from the death penalty to life imprisonment without the possibility of being released back into society on parole.

I found this theory very interesting. If we successfully argued this particular issue, then Mattson would be spared the death penalty while serving out his sentence in prison. Clearly, this would resolve my own personal dilemma. Life imprisonment without the possibility of parole would mean that at least our professional obligations toward Mattson would have been satisfied. As a result of Ron's work, Mattson would be off death row. This relieved my conscience.

My mood changed, though, when Ron finished telling me what he had found and asked me for the results of my own review of the documents. I was stunned. Ron had not mentioned finding the issue that I had discovered. This put me in a somewhat awkward position. I had spent so much time dealing with my conflicted feelings because I thought that I had found an issue that ultimately could result in Mattson's conviction being reversed, yet Ron had not even brought it up. I was the student, and Ron was the mentor. I was supposed to be learning from him. How could I diplomatically tell Ron that I might have found a potentially larger issue that he himself had overlooked?

Ron could see by my facial expression that something was wrong.

"Hey, Jim—what's up?" he asked, frowning. "You don't agree?"

"No, no—you're right, of course. The judge was wrong."

I then explained that I had discovered what I believed was a second issue, one that might reverse Mattson's conviction altogether. Ron stared at me for a moment. Then his response broke the silence.

"Are you kidding? What are you talking about?" he asked with a hearty laugh.

"Ron, I'm serious," I repeated, somewhat embarrassed by his laughter.

"You're *serious*," he retorted, taken aback.

When he realized that I was, he stopped smiling and asked me more specifically what issue I had uncovered.

"Mattson's rights were violated by the actions of Detective Dingle of the North Las Vegas Police Department," I said, "as well as by Detective Reed of the Los Angeles County Sheriff's Department."

I explored the specific facts that I felt were contrary to California law and the U.S. Constitution. I explained that I believed that the confessions Mattson gave to Detective Dingle and later to Detective Reed of the Los Angeles County Sheriff's Department were illegally obtained. In both cases, Mattson had been read his rights but had been questioned outside the presence of counsel. It was my position that an individual is most vulnerable to breaking down when he is alone without any support mechanism to guide him through the interrogation process. Dingle, I believed, had deliberately formed a bond with Mattson to lure him into a false sense of security. Supporting this position was the fact that Mattson would only meet with California law enforcement personnel if Dingle agreed to be in the interrogation room at the same time. After I finished, Ron examined me with a stern look on his face.

"Jim, I think that's a stretch. Mattson was read his rights, and on more than one occasion, I might add."

"That might be," I replied. "However, once he invoked his rights *the first time*, I believe they should have refrained from asking him anything else without the benefit of counsel!"

Looking over his horn-rimmed glasses, he replied to my more serious demeanor, "I don't agree with your analysis of the facts, but I respect your opinion enough to have you research it out. If you can support your position with facts, legal principles, and case law, I will include it in the brief."

"Fair enough," I replied with a smile I could not contain. My adrenaline was rising. I love a challenge and Ron had just given me a big one. I had fought with my feelings to reach this level but now that I was there, I was not going to be deterred. I was pretty sure that I was correct. More importantly, I did take pride in the work that I had done. I had put in an ungodly amount of time already, and moving forward was the only reasonable course of action.

Although I was pleased with Ron's response, a sinking feeling started to take root almost at once in the pit of my stomach. The issue had now fallen back on me. There was no easy way out unless my research determined that I had been incorrect. If I turned out to be right, I would be releasing a predator back onto the streets of California to potentially rape and kill again.

After leaving Ron's office, I drove home and thought about the course of events that had occupied my mind over the past few weeks. At a minimum, I knew Ron depended on me to assist him, and Mattson, in his death row prison cell, would be relying on a defense team that would hopefully get his conviction either reversed or at least move him off death row. It was time for me to concentrate on the details of the case and on the issue I had determined to be significant in light of the facts surrounding Mattson's incarceration in Nevada. It was clear to me at the time that in order to be fully focused on my objective, I would have to put my personal repugnance, as well as my ethics, on hold. Any objective we seek to accomplish, from the smallest task to a major event in our lives, ought to be performed to the best of our abilities. I was reminded of something my mother had constantly emphasized to all her children: "Anything worth doing is worth doing right."

With that thought in mind, I knew what had to be done, and I dove into my research with a maximum effort.

EIGHT

KEEPING THE FOCUS

Since I had already finished reading and reviewing all the trial transcripts and exhibits, determining my course of action became simple. It began with my examination of Mattson's arrest. Sheriff Robinson had in fact advised him of his rights at the time he was picked up at his grandparents' house in Cherry Creek. When Dingle and King picked Mattson up and drove him the three hours to North Las Vegas, they also advised him of his rights, and did not question him after he asked for an attorney. This did not seem like it would be an issue for the appeal.

<hr />

After hours sitting at my desk going through the same information over and over again, I needed a break and time to digest the information. I got up from my desk and took a walk around the neighborhood to clear my head. We lived on a street that was always alive with children's activity. As I walked along, I could see boys and girls laughing and having the type of fun kids should be having. My mind drifted to the girls whose young lives had been interrupted by Mattson. Their fun and innocence was over. Walking back into my house, I had to remind myself what my ultimate objective was. I could not let myself be distracted by my personal feelings. It was critical to the case that I maintain my focus.

Walking past our bedroom, I took a moment to peek in on Betty and Jamal. They were napping, which was a relief since it gave me more time to work before the afternoon ebbed into the daily routine of preparing dinner. Back at my desk, I settled in for the long haul. Within a few minutes, my mind was back in North Las Vegas.

———◦◦◦———

After Mattson arrived in North Las Vegas, he was subsequently brought before a judge and made aware of the charges being levied against him. After this arraignment, the Public Defender's Office appointed an attorney to represent Mattson to safeguard his rights during all the critical stages of the judicial process, which included interrogation by law enforcement.

The first set of facts that piqued my interest was the fact that it was Mattson who had initiated the conversation with Dingle that created this ongoing relationship between the two men. It appeared that Dingle had only gone along with this relationship because he hoped to lull Mattson into a false sense of security so Mattson would talk to him and confess to committing the crimes. Without the presence of counsel, this course of behavior is contrary to the rights given to Americans by the Sixth Amendment.

———◈———

Betty entered the room, interrupting my concentration.

"How's it coming along?"

"Pretty good," I responded, distracted, my head still buried in the transcripts and documents.

"You look puzzled. What's wrong?" Betty asked.

"Actually, nothing is wrong, but in reading over this stuff, it appears that the detective and Mattson began feeling a little *too* at ease with each other."

"So, what's wrong with that?" Betty asked, shrugging her shoulders.

"I think the problem was the officer. Based on the relationship that was apparently developing between the two, he began to have casual coffee meetings with Mattson." I took off my glasses and rubbed my eyes. "As a result, he asked Mattson questions about other crimes that he allegedly might have committed in California."

"I still don't understand. What's *wrong* with that?" Betty sat down on my office couch, looking legitimately confused.

"Honestly, I don't know. But I have a hunch that Dingle—that's the detective—may have been casually interrogating Mattson without his attorney being present, which would clearly be a violation of his constitutional rights," I responded.

"Huh, don't cops do that all the time?" Betty quipped. "It wouldn't be a first, would it?"

Her statement was sincere. Although she'd been born in New Orleans, her family had relocated to Los Angeles, where she'd found growing up in South Central challenging. The community and its relationship with the Los Angeles Police Department were such that she had a dim view of law enforcement and the manner in which they treated suspects. My relationship with authorities growing up had been completely different, considering my little town only had one part-time police officer whom everyone knew and respected.

"Well, I don't know about that, but at the moment, my concern is that any time Dingle started to have these conversations, he always read Mattson his rights first."

With that response, I once again became absorbed in my thoughts, and did not even notice when Betty left the room.

⸻⬦⸻

Yet, realistically, how many times does a suspect have his or her rights read before he or she caves in under the pressure and agrees to talk? I asked myself, playing devil's advocate to my own argument.

Whatever that magic number was, Mattson had finally waived his rights and agreed to talk to Dingle regarding the offenses committed against Kiz Livingston in California.

Mattson opened up and began discussing details, and Dingle was, of course, all ears. Throughout this process, and unbeknown to Mattson, it had been Dingle's mindset to assist Detective Branch of the Huntington Beach Police Department in obtaining as much information as possible. Mattson explained to Dingle in one of their many conversations that he had been staying with his sister at the time of the attack and had started out early in the morning "cruising for a woman." After Mattson was finished with his description of the facts, the suspect signed a transcribed version of his statement.

During similar conversations, Mattson explained to Dingle that he had kidnapped, raped, sodomized, and killed other girls, even though Dingle and the authorities were unaware of those cases at that time. He further commented that the reason he had killed his victims was because he did not want any of them to be able to go to court and testify against him as Jeanette had in Oregon. He did not want to go back to prison. Mattson also indicated that he was responsible for the Gutierrez homicide, as well as another one that would later turn out to be the Corradini killing.

By this time, the investigation conducted by the North Las Vegas Police Department regarding the kidnapping and rape of the Nevada girl, Sonia Lindsey, had been completed. Any further interrogation by Dingle for any Nevada crimes would not have been necessary to convict Mattson. As a result, Mattson's attorney, Rick Ahlswede, did not object to further discussions between Mattson and Dingle because his client had already confessed to the crimes he had committed against Sonia. Although Mattson's public defender knew that his client was a suspect for felony sex crimes in California, he had no knowledge that his client was also a murder suspect there.

Mattson's Nevada attorney had been too cavalier in permitting law enforcement personnel to question his client without his being present. It almost appeared as though he did not care since he was finished representing Mattson in the Nevada case. Even so, he probably should have advised Mattson not to say anything to the police about any of the California crimes, regardless of what those crimes actually were. A good criminal defense attorney believes in the old adage, "Keep your mouth shut. Don't volunteer any information," and is always present for any interrogation of his or her client.

Ahlswede's attitude may have created another problem. On or about November 8, 1978, Dingle permitted Mattson to be interviewed by Detective Reed of the Los Angeles County Sheriff's Department, who had contacted Dingle earlier concerning the murder of 9-year-old Cheryl Gutierrez. Reed had called the Public Defender's Office in an effort to reach Ahlswede to obtain his consent to interrogate Mattson and to see whether he had any objections. Unable to reach him, and without any further attempt to contact a supervisor or any other member of the Public Defender's Office, Reed commenced his interrogation of Mattson with only Dingle's permission as the senior detective in charge of Mattson and anyone wishing to question him.

During this conversation, Reed identified why he was there. He specifically told Mattson he wanted to talk to him regarding a murder that had taken place in Santa Fe Springs, California. Mattson looked at Reed and said, "You mean, the little girl." Reed replied in the affirmative and asked Mattson what he knew about her.

Mattson responded, "Just what I heard or read."

Reed retorted, "Michael, I think you know more than that."

When Mattson asked Reed why he thought that, Reed told Mattson that he had been seen at Santa Fe Springs High School by a janitor who had recognized Mattson as a former student at Legg Junior High School where the witness had previously worked. Mattson, upon being told this crucial information, looked at Reed and declared, "Well, then you know about it."

Mattson broke down at that point and began to give Reed the intricate details of the murder—details that had not been printed in any newspaper and could only have been known by the killer. If Ahlswede had been present at this interrogation like he should have been, he never would have allowed Mattson to make this confession.

Wanting to ensure that they were both speaking about the same person, Reed showed Mattson a photograph of little Cheryl Gutierrez before she was killed. According to Reed's later testimony, Mattson immediately pushed it away and became "rather violent about it," eventually stating, "I will tell you one that you do not even know about."

The conversation then took another direction as Mattson described the events surrounding the kidnapping, rape, sodomy, and brutal murder of Adele Corradini. To confirm to Reed that he was being on the "up and up," Mattson directed the California detective to where he could find a map showing the whereabouts of Adele's remains. The map was in Mattson's impounded Plymouth and was recovered by Dingle and Reed.

Mattson, intentionally or by accident, had not only confessed to the crimes against Cheryl, Adele, and Kiz, but had also given hard evidence that he, in fact, had committed these crimes—all without the presence of counsel, and more than likely because of the personal relationship he had established with Dingle.

In my mind, the protections afforded to each citizen, such as the right against self-incrimination and the right to counsel, were called into question by the circumstances surrounding Mattson's admissions. There had to be a concern that a suspect's rights may have been violated if detectives continued to interrogate him after he initially stated that he did not want to speak to law enforcement and wished to talk to an attorney—even if his rights were read each time. Both Dingle and Reed mentioned that Mattson had been interrogated on numerous occasions outside the presence of counsel. Furthermore, a suspect or defendant could legitimately break down and begin to speak even after he had been advised of his rights if continued pressure were exerted on that individual to talk. Dingle, by establishing a casual relationship with Mattson, did not remove the possibility that Mattson might have felt under duress as he freely began opening up about his crime spree.

NINE

FAMILY VERSUS ETHICS

"Daddy, wake up!"

This was a familiar sound on Saturday mornings. Jamal never minded waking me up when he knew I did not have to go to work. Unfortunately, getting back to sleep was next to impossible. He would jump up and down on the bed until I gave him the attention he desperately wanted. Betty and I had decided before Jamal was born that she would stay at home with him until he was ready for preschool. As a result, she spent a considerable amount of time with him, but I was not around as much because of my very hectic schedule.

"Jamal," I muttered, removing the covers from over my head, "let Daddy get some sleep."

He had no idea that I had been up most of the night.

"Mommy says get up," he replied, continuing his trampoline routine.

Before I could answer him, Betty entered the room. She was already dressed, and by her attire, I remembered that I had promised her I would set aside that particular Saturday to take the family to the Los Angeles Zoo since Jamal had never been there. What she didn't know was that I had resolved the night before that my preplanned Saturday would have to be canceled so I could spend more time at the library, once again.

"Jimi, c'mon and get up. You promised we were going to take Jamal to the zoo today."

As she lifted our son up from the bed, she immediately recognized, by the expression on my face, that my plans had changed.

"Do *not* tell me that you are going to let this boy down again!" she shouted.

"Betty, I have to go to the library to do some research on Mattson's case. I'm running out of time, and I have to follow up on some things that I came across last night."

The look on her face said it all. I could only stare back at her. She was mad as hell. This was not the first time that I had pulled the rug out from under her, changing our plans due to work, school, or Mattson's case. I avoided looking at Jamal. He knew enough to understand that we were not going to the zoo, and this made my heart sink, but I could not avoid it. I had a job to do.

"Jimi, this is getting old real fast," she remarked.

With that comment, Betty left the room. I stared up at the ceiling for a long time and finally decided that I had to maintain my focus. After slipping into some clothes, I gathered my research materials and packed my briefcase. Betty was in the living room with Jamal, watching cartoons. Passing through the living room on my way out the front door, I glanced over at Betty.

"See you later," I stated in a very nonchalant manner, addressing both of them.

I didn't get an answer, nor had I expected one. All eyes remained averted. As I left, I decided I would have to make this up to both her and Jamal later.

The trip to the library gave me a chance to clear my head. I reached the downtown branch of the Los Angeles Public Library in what seemed to be a very short period of time. It was a huge library, but I could always get a rough idea as to the number of people inside by the amount of cars parked in the lot outside. I hated waiting for resource materials that were already in use.

Having a clear understanding of the charges Mattson had been convicted of gave me a clear blueprint for proceeding. Every law student, law clerk, and lawyer has the dreaded responsibility of researching cases to support his or her position. Having spent more hours in the law library than I can count, I was not intimidated by the process. However, this set of circumstances was completely different. A man's life hung in the balance.

Unfortunately, my hopes were dashed that day. I did not find any cases to support my theory, and upon leaving the library, I regretted not fulfilling the promise to my family about going to the zoo.

I continued my daily trek to the library the following week. Each visit, as usual, began with a mutual nod of good morning with the librarian, accompanied by a certain amount of displeasure with myself. I was not pleased that I was unable to find any case that supported my theory. On the third day, I really became irritated. I was tired, it was getting late, and I had not even stopped to eat lunch. I decided I would give it one more shot before I left. I switched my focus from murder convictions to other types of convictions involving confessions that had been obtained during an interrogation initiated by law enforcement. The computer kicked a case citation back to me entitled *The People v. Frank J. Pettingill*, a California case out of Santa Barbara County.

I began to read the case with a little bit of skepticism, since I had run into so many brick walls previously. Within a few moments, though, my attitude changed. I straightened up in my chair, and with every word I read, the excitement began to build within me. I was like a thermometer, quickly rising from zero to ninety, all in a few seconds. I read on, excited.

The facts were intriguing, but more importantly, they were similar in nature to Mattson's case. The issues came clearly into view, and after a couple hours of reading, I knew I was on the right track. I had struck gold! I jumped up from my chair and in my excitement, knocked it over. The sound of it crashing to the floor echoed against the high ceilings.

I regained my focus and left shortly thereafter. On my drive home, I began to compare the case I discovered in the library that day with Mattson's. Pettingill's confession had been obtained during an interrogation initiated by law enforcement officers after Pettingill twice refused to waive his privilege against self-incrimination. In both of these cases, the defendants were always read their rights prior to being questioned. The similarities were indeed remarkable.

My thoughts carried me home in what felt like a very short drive. Darkness had fallen and I knew Jamal would be sleeping. I arrived home and found Betty stretched out on the living room couch. It was more comfortable for her as she got closer to her due date.

"How you doin'?" I asked.

My concern was real, and I could tell it was appreciated. I am sure she had begun to feel as though my only interest was for my research. She returned the kindness by showing a little of her own.

"Oh, I'm fine. Just relaxing before I turn in. How's the research coming along?"

I was glad that she had asked. Her inquiry gave me a chance to discuss some key issues out loud. By now I had taken a seat in my favorite easy chair and was ready to unload.

Over the next hour, I recapped what I had found at the library and told her about the similarities between the two cases. Although Betty had no legal background, she clearly understood my point that each of the defendants had confessed to other crimes after having told their interrogators that they did not want to answer any questions without their lawyer being there. In her mind, though, Mattson was still a murderer and a predator of children, which meant he belonged in jail; however, she did acknowledge that any police interrogations that went beyond their legal rights were wrong.

We talked well into the night, which was something that we had not done in a long time. At the end of the night, we both agreed that neither of us would change our positions regarding Mattson. Betty eventually got up from the couch and went to bed. I was left alone with my thoughts. I still had a lot to figure out. I reasoned that the court would have to scrutinize the behavior of the police officers conducting the interrogation, even if those officers were from another law enforcement agency and dealt with crimes different from those for which the defendant had initially been arrested. Pettingill had been interrogated by two different law enforcement agencies, both from California. Mattson, on the other hand, had been questioned by police officers from two different agencies within Nevada and by several agencies from California.

I thought about Mattson and put myself in his shoes. My position was simple. Once a suspect declared that he wished to assert his privilege against self-incrimination, it was unlawful for *any* law enforcement agency to continue or renew the interrogation process, and any statement elicited thereafter should have been inadmissible, since the defendant had asserted his right to remain silent.

The next day I awakened very early and went to see Ron, hoping his expertise as a former deputy district attorney would help me. I was curious as to whether or not I was heading in the right direction with my research, and I needed reassurance. I was very happy to find him in his office so early. We discussed my position. Ron listened intently and stated, "Jim, arguably, the facts you have outlined could be considered coercive, especially without the presence of counsel."

I was relieved to hear that he agreed. We also discussed that such a setting, with its subtle pressures of unfamiliar surroundings, physical and psychological isolation, and a police-dominated atmosphere, could all be factors in determining whether a confession was ultimately judged to be coerced. We talked for awhile and concluded our conversation with the understanding that I was heading in the right direction.

I arrived back home around breakfast time and was greeted by Jamal. He was always happy to see me walk through the door. Betty was glad that I'd made it home in time to eat breakfast with her and Jamal. She believed in the family life, and cherished the time we spent together when I was available. But our breakfast conversation ended up being very short once I announced I had to head back to the library. She was not happy with the prospect, but by this time she knew I was closing in on my deadlines for Ron.

After I finished eating, I gathered up my things, including the binders with Dingle's testimony, and headed back down to the library. It was a place of solitude and I was grateful that it stayed open late. I retreated to my favorite spot and pulled out the transcripts with Dingle's testimony. It was important to have the facts right in order to compare them to the cases that I had found. This whole business of whether Mattson waived his right to counsel or whether Dingle mislead Mattson based upon their relationship was critical to the appeal.

In his court testimony, Dingle took the position that he was approached by Mattson and, as a result, Mattson opened the door to having "conversations."

> **FELDMAN:** As those five participants in the lineup, the people that stood in the lineup were being escorted away from the lineup, did something— were you approached by anybody from that lineup?

> **DINGLE:** Yes. Mike Mattson.

FELDMAN: What transpired? What occurred?

DINGLE: As they were proceeding from that lineup room through the detective bureau, Mike held back and let another prisoner walk in front of him, and he got my attention as he passed through my area. He just looked at me and said, "I'd like to talk to you." A short time later the jailer put him in the interrogation room and I met with him.

FELDMAN: He asked you—is the first thing he asked you, where his car was?

DINGLE: That's what I recall.

FELDMAN: Did you tell him where his car was?

DINGLE: Yes, that we impounded it.

FELDMAN: Did you ask him if he wanted to have an attorney present for any further conversations?

DINGLE: I did at the outset as part of the rights and waiver, but no, not throughout—

FELDMAN: Not again?

DINGLE: Not throughout the conversation. No.

FELDMAN: So it was only after you got into this conversation and began talking to him that some of the facts of the crime began to come out; is that right?

DINGLE: At one point, yes, we started talking, going from a general conversation into the investigation.

FELDMAN: Do you recall whether you asked him specific questions?

DINGLE: A specific question?

FELDMAN: It's possible for a question about the facts of the crime at some point in the conversation.

DINGLE: I did, yes.

This piece of the testimony was critical. Dingle admitted that he did begin to ask specific questions about the crimes in question. Mattson made a general inquiry regarding the whereabouts of his vehicle. The problem that was later established in more detail was that Dingle used this opportunity to begin a casual relationship with Mattson. Continuing to read him his rights did not negate the reality that he was interrogating him outside the presence of counsel.

———◦———

I left the library and walked outside. It was late, and an evening breeze brought about a calmness within me. I had just about come to the end of my journey. I felt it was appropriate to celebrate. I drove to the local liquor store and picked up a bottle of champagne.

When I got home, Betty and Jamal had just finished eating dinner and I gave my usual greetings. Betty fixed me a plate of greens, macaroni and cheese, and fried chicken. Definitely one of my favorite meals, and I was starving. I had been at the library practically all day and had never left to eat.

"Thanks, looks great! How was your day?" I asked her.

"Not bad, I took Jamal to the park. He loved it." Eyeing the champagne, she pointed and wondered, "What's the occasion?"

"Well," I said, swallowing a mouthful of macaroni, "it was a good day of research. I found cases that support my contention that Mattson's rights were violated. I think I'm basically done with my research, depending on what Ron decides."

"What *Ron* decides? What about what *you* decide?" She placed her elbows on the table and looked at me over the top of her glasses with a disapproving look.

"What do you mean by that? Ron is the supervising attorney, and he gets to make the call on all of this. It's not my decision." I continued eating, trying to enjoy my dinner.

"Jimi, you know what I'm talking about! You are giving him information that you feel will help set that idiot free. I know how hard you've worked on this. But you also know how I feel about all of this. Simply tell him you didn't find anything!"

I sat back in my chair and stared at her. I could not believe what I was hearing. I had worked hard on this case, and I was not about to deceive Ron about the results of my research. Furthermore, Ron would probably think I was a fool if I came to him looking like I had not done any work on the case.

"I can't do that. I won't do that." I set my plate aside and glared at her.

"You and your goddamn *principles*! You wanna celebrate, go ahead, but do not expect me to join in!"

Having made her point abundantly clear, Betty got up from the table, lifted Jamal up from his seat, and went upstairs, mumbling all the way.

As I finished my dinner, I stared at the bottle of Brut champagne that had just been transformed from a symbol of celebration to a line drawn in the sand. Betty's refusal to celebrate was understandable because her perspective was typical of the average citizen who does not want a sexual predator back on the loose. But what about her role as my wife? Wasn't she supposed to be supportive of the spouse who had just had a major breakthrough in his work? What might that do for her young husband's budding career?

I decided to drink my bottle of champagne because I felt that I deserved it. When I had finished the bottle, I decided to confront Betty. She had just put Jamal to bed.

"Betty, could I speak with you in my study?" I yelled upstairs.

"Be right down," she replied.

Betty appeared a few minutes later and saw the empty champagne bottle turned upside down in the ice bucket. "I see you didn't save *me* any," she remarked in a tone dripping with sarcasm.

"Didn't think you wanted any," I replied in a manner equal to the comment I had received.

Betty, recognizing that I was upset about her lack of support, began discussing why she felt the way she did. It was simple enough to understand. She did not feel that sexual predators and murderers deserved another opportunity to prey on children and women. Having a child of her own and another on the way made her highly sensitive to the issues involving Mattson.

I listened patiently, but I honestly felt she was over-looking my professional career path for which, quite frankly, we had both made huge sacrifices. Having nothing to lose and everything to gain, I reasoned that the only solution was to express my viewpoints in greater detail. Sighing with frustration, I went back to the basics.

"Betty, when Ron first called me to help him, do you recall how we were *both* excited about the opportunity that was being presented to me?"

"Yep, and what about it?" She peered at me quizzically.

"At that time, neither of us knew the details of the case. We reasoned that the individual in question, meaning Mattson, had obviously killed someone, but each of us, for our own reasons, I'm sure, viewed the opportunity as a great experience for me. I was not any less upset than you were when I learned about the details of the crimes Mattson had committed. You remember how I fought with my inner feelings for the longest time in an effort to come up with a workable mental solution."

"Yes. But if *you* recall when you *did* tell me about what that guy had done, I was against your doing anything to help him, and my feelings have not changed." Her nostrils flared. "So do *not* come to me with a bottle of champagne, asking me to help you celebrate an event that has no meaning to me under the circumstances. I hope they fry the bastard!"

"Betty, you were against me helping him, but *only* after you found out he was a sexual predator," I shot back.

"And?" She quipped.

"Well, initially, it was you who mentioned to me that at a minimum, the guy had to have been a murderer, or otherwise he would not have been given the death penalty! Are you saying it's okay to get *another* kind of murderer off, but not Mattson?"

"Jimi, if *you* don't know the difference between types of killers, I don't know what to say!" I could only stare at her. I could not argue with her point, and there was no reason to try to convince her that my way of thinking was superior to hers. Representing Mattson after having found out the reason for his conviction had been my dilemma from the start of the case, and I should not have expected to sway her emotions just because I was her husband.

The silence was broken by Betty. "Anything else?" she asked, her voice a steel door.

"Nope. I think you've expressed your opinion on the subject, and I doubt that we need to discuss this again," I quietly replied.

Betty left and went back upstairs, her posture stiff with suppressed outrage.

I sat in my recliner, looking around the room at some of the highlights of my life that were reflected in picture frames and small statuettes displayed on the different bookshelves. My eyes fell on my Eagle Scout award. Some of the principles that were so entrenched in me had been developed during the time I was working toward that achievement. It seemed like ages ago. I remembered my Board of Review, which had been a committee of adults who interviewed each scout prior to being approved to become an Eagle Scout. They had asked me what my intended career path was. That answer had been simple: I wanted to be a lawyer. I had always wanted to be one.

At that moment, I consciously decided I would focus on my agenda for this case and that from there on out, I would no longer discuss my involvement with Mattson's appeal with anyone but Ron.

My attention gradually turned back to the business at hand. I was part of a defense team, and I could not afford to become sidetracked by personal emotions. I had been down that road and was not going back. I had made up my mind to do the best job I could, and I intended to pursue my quest. I had found evidence that supported my argument, and I was going to take the evidence to Ron to build the strongest case for our client that I could. I went to bed with that thought in mind.

I got up pretty early the next morning and retreated to my study. A modest room, consisting of my mauve recliner, a roll-top desk and matching high-backed chair, a television, and bookshelves packed with a variety of books, pictures, and assorted family memorabilia, it was my sanctuary.

I began reviewing the transcripts and facts in comparison to the two cases I had found. I was satisfied that I had the right cases but also recognized that my job was far from over. My thought process was interrupted by a knock on the door and a figure entering the room. It was Betty.

"Jimi, we need to talk."

Her face was grim, which immediately told me the conversation from the night before was not over.

"About what?" I knew the answer already.

She came in and sat down in my recliner. It was early, and she was still bundled up in her oversized bathrobe and fluffy slippers.

"If I am not mistaken, you told me that guy confessed to raping and killing those girls."

"Yeah, he did."

"Well, why do you want to help him get off?" She waved her hands in the air.

"Betty, *why* are you so fixated on this issue?" The tone in my voice clearly indicated that I was getting annoyed.

"I honestly do *not* feel that people like that should be out on the street. He's right where he needs to be, and

I do *not* like the idea that you are helping him. I'm sorry, but that's how I feel!" Her cheeks looked flushed.

"Look, Betty," I said, leaning forward in my chair, "I don't like what this guy did any more than you. The reality is, *I have a job to do!* I gave Ron my word that I would help him. Admittedly, I did not know what Mattson had done when I first took this on. I was sickened to read about the different things he did to those girls."

I was up on my feet by this time, pacing back and forth as if I were pleading a case before a jury. Why not? I definitely had a captive audience.

"We have a system of justice in this country," I continued, "that basically gives every citizen certain rights when they are either arrested or tried for crimes they are alleged to have committed. Police officers, in the performance of their job, are held to a high standard because they are the individuals with the responsibility to uphold the law. It's not for *them* to determine who is guilty or innocent. Their job is simply to make the arrest and, in doing so, ensure the rights of the suspect."

"*Their* rights!" Betty retorted. "What about the *rights* of those girls and their families?"

"I agree with you! Your concerns are the same as mine. I want *every* victim, no matter the crime committed against them, to have the person who committed the act pay for his or her deeds." I paused for a moment to see if she was truly listening. She was, so I kept going. "Betty, you have to understand that the only way any of us can be assured that *everyone's* rights are protected—whether it applies to the victims, their families, or, yes, even the rights of a suspect—is for the police to do their job properly. When they take it upon themselves to violate the rights of the individuals they arrest, everyone loses. Wouldn't you agree?"

"*Of course* I agree. Try to explain that logic to the brothers being arrested in South Central every day! Nobody seems to care whether or not *their* rights are being violated." She was on my side on this point and I felt a breath of fresh air.

"I am as concerned about their rights as you are, and that is *exactly* why I am going to do everything I can to get Mattson's conviction overturned."

"I did not know he was black," Betty replied, a surprised look on her face.

"He's not—he's white." I paused, wondering if she would feel differently if my client were, in fact, a brother. I chose to proceed. "The point I'm trying to make is, we cannot look at the judicial system as being *anything other than neutral.* As a society, we have to apply our laws to everyone, regardless of an individual's race or the crimes they commit."

"Jimi, you sound like a poster boy for law and order!"

With that comment, Betty got up and started to leave the room. She stopped and turned back.

"I know you are a well-principled man, Jimi. It's one of the reasons I married you. I'm also aware that when you have your mind made up about something, there is nothing, nor anyone in this world, that can make you change your mind. You do what you feel you have to do."

After Betty's departure, I was once again alone with my thoughts. All this aggravation for a man I had never even met. My mind shifted over to Ron. I wondered how he coped with such issues. He had been a prosecutor for Riverside County at one time. Putting criminals in jail would certainly be different from getting them out. Another mind-set, for sure. It was still somewhat early, but I decided to call him.

"Hello." It was Ron.

"Ron, sorry to call so early, but I need to talk to you."

"No problem, Jim. What's on your mind?"

"I've had several discussions with Betty about this case we're working on, and she's not very happy about my helping Mattson get off. She thinks Mattson is right where he belongs. I tried to explain to her that it's our responsibility to represent him to the best of our ability without giving any consideration to the crimes he committed."

"Well, that's true. It *is* our responsibility, both professionally and ethically. You want me to talk to her?"

I hesitated. "No. But I do wonder how you cope with this burden. I mean, I'm doing all of this for a guy I've never met, and you've been at it for years. You've met Mattson. What's he like? *Is* he worth saving?" I leaned back in my chair expectantly.

I knew the answer: *It's not whether or not he's worth saving. One has nothing to do with the other*. I was more curious about Mattson, however. Ron had just gotten back from visiting him at San Quentin, and we had not had a chance to talk about his visit. Now he told me.

"Jim, take it from me with my years of experience. It's never an issue as to the crimes these individuals commit. Our job is never to judge. We represent people because they are entitled to representation. You see, society in general would agree with that statement; however, when *they* become victims, most people forget about the rights that are afforded to their assailant. It's understandable."

"Yeah, I do understand that. But tell me about Mattson. What was he like?"

"Honestly, there's not much to tell. I was in a small room that was very hot. One wall was half glass, with a counter and telephone. The same was visible from the other side. Mattson appeared, dressed in a gray shirt and pants. He has a very small physical frame. I was honestly surprised. I would have thought he'd be bigger, considering what he did to those girls. He had long dark hair, and was clean-shaven. We actually did not discuss much. It was really only intended as a 'meet and greet' and to inform him that his appeal was moving forward. He was a soft-spoken guy, and really, that's about it. I don't think the entire meeting lasted more than twenty minutes or so." I could almost hear Ron shaking his head.

"Well, at a minimum, I hope he appreciated what we're doing for him," I replied.

"Who knows? How's the research coming since we last spoke?"

I explained that I was very pleased and was continuing in an effort to tie up some loose ends. We agreed to meet the next day at his office so I could show him what I had found.

The next day, at last, I was ready to present my findings to Ron. I had my issues, as well as my supporting case law and legal principles. In addition, my position was supported by the California Constitution. My only concern was whether Ron would buy into my argument that Dingle's conduct, as a facilitator between Mattson and the various California law enforcement agencies, would have the legal effect of having become an agent of those agencies. As such, Dingle would therefore be held to the same standards as any other California law enforcement detective. Reed's out-of-state conduct, I knew, would be an easier sell. California law should apply to law enforcement personnel when working in that capacity in another state.

I drove to Ron's Beverly Hills office with a smile on my face. I was elated. My inner struggle was over and I was confident my original assessment that Mattson's rights were violated was correct. When I met with Ron, however, he was somewhat skeptical.

"Jim, I read over the transcripts again. I am still convinced that all of the proper procedures were followed. It's clear from the record that Mattson confessed *after* he had been given his rights on several occasions! I simply don't see what point you are trying to drive here."

I rose to my feet and walked over to his office window, which held a view that overlooked the city. I was calm and sure of my findings. I turned around and faced my mentor.

"Ron," I replied, "I agree that he confessed after having been read his rights. The problem, as I see it, is that Mattson may have been pressured into confessing by Dingle's continued interrogations *after* he lulled Mattson into a casual friendship."

My statement having been made, I returned to my seat.

"A casual friendship?" Ron sat back in his chair and stared at me for what seemed like an eternity. "Explain that."

"Okay. Remember that Dingle and Mattson would have coffee meetings together. These interactions came after Mattson initially indicated he did not want to speak with Dingle and wanted the benefit of counsel. As time went on, they continued to meet after he confessed to the Nevada crime, which is not our concern here. The meetings became very casual and Mattson, as a result, became really comfortable interacting with Dingle, to the point where he requested that Dingle sit in on all of the interviews between Mattson and other law enforcement agencies that Dingle began to arrange."

Now it was my turn to sit back. Ron took off his glasses and rose from his chair. Walking over to the window, it was his turn to absorb the view. It was easy to see he was deep in thought. Ron was a tough sell. Even though we had discussed the issues before, he still had a problem with the fact that Mattson had been read his rights *every* time he spoke with law enforcement officers. I understood his point. Part of the problem was that Ron was still focused on his own issue. He was convinced that the major error was that the court had given the wrong jury instruction, and Mattson should have received life imprisonment without the possibility of parole. As a law clerk, I knew my responsibility was merely one of support, but I had made a number of personal sacrifices throughout the many weeks I had been working on this project. I wasn't going to let go of the issues that I had found and worked on without a fight! On the other hand, I also knew Ron well enough to know how far I could push my own argument. I may have been his law clerk, but I was also his friend, and that relationship wasn't going to be tainted because of these issues. As a professor and mentor, he was very patient and listened to every point of view. I waited for a second opportunity to argue my perspective further. I sat there like a race horse waiting for that bell to sound the start of the race.

Ron returned to his seat and we discussed every other aspect of the case, as well as other potential concerns that were also worth considering. We discussed the facts and each supporting case in great detail. This is not an unusual approach. Normally, when a case is appealed, every possible issue is submitted with the hope that one of those appealed may be sufficient for a favorable verdict, resulting in a reversal of the lower court's decision. After we finished discussing Ron's issues—of which there were ten—the focus once again turned toward my argument. Ron had given it some thought and decided to include it in the brief that we would write and submit to the California Supreme Court, admitting that he felt my argument had merit. I jumped up from my seat and enthusiastically shook his hand using both of mine. I felt like I had passed his course all over again. More importantly, I took his acceptance as a further acknowledgment of my contribution. I had put so much time and energy, into this project that I didn't want my efforts to be for naught.

I left his office after promising I would call him back to give him a date and time for our next dinner engagement with our wives. Considering all the time that I had spent away from Betty, I was highly motivated to make the plans. It would at least be a first step in the journey back to normalcy.

TEN

THE APPEAL

The research was completed. The think tank was closed. It was time to write the brief. This part of the appeal process was left entirely to Ron. I had submitted my findings and the cases that backed them up. As the attorney of record, Ron had the responsibility to write and submit the brief to the California Supreme Court for the justices' consideration. The brief contained thirteen issues. Ten of those issues were those that Ron had developed, and the other three were based solely upon my research.

Ron completed the first draft within two weeks and sent me a copy so I could review the portions that pertained to my issues. He wanted to make sure that he had captured my argument, even though he was not in full agreement. Up until that moment, I had been able to relax and spend some quality time with my family. That night after dinner, I sat down and read the brief. When I finished, I felt a sense of relief that the journey had almost come to an end. The last piece of the puzzle was going to be whether or not the California Supreme Court justices agreed with any of our arguments and would reverse Mattson's conviction. At the very least, I was happy that I no longer had to worry about my struggles, the research, the impassioned arguments with Betty, and my absences from Jamal.

Our finished "Appellant's Opening Brief" was submitted to the clerk on August 4, 1982. Ninety days later, Ron argued the case before the highest court in California. Dressed in a dark pinstripe suit, he entered the courtroom with a look of determination without any outward sign of being nervous. He had argued before judges and juries in more cases than he could probably remember, but this day was different from the rest. It was the first time he would present an argument before the California Supreme Court, and we both hoped he would be able to successfully hold his ground against their questions.

Ron carefully removed his folder from his black brief-case. He was seated at a desk by the podium. I could see him deep in thought as he flipped the pages to ensure he was prepared. I knew he was ready. The courtroom gradually began to fill with spectators, as well as opposing counsel on behalf of the People. They took their places on the other side of the railing.

Ron went through the brief he had written, explaining the most important points, and building his argument to convince the justices to either over-turn the sentence of death or, even better, to overturn the conviction itself.

Among the number of other arguments we had care-fully crafted, Ron made the argument I had seen the first time I read through all the files, back at the begin-ning of my participation in the case. Ron pointed out that after Mattson was first advised of his rights by Detective Dingle and Mattson requested counsel, no further questioning related to crimes of any sort should have been conducted without Mattson's lawyer being in the room.

Ron looked squarely at the justices as he spoke.

> How many times should a person be required to assert his rights before the police are required to listen? Does it matter if the police officer is from Nevada or California when that officer reopens the dialogue previously closed by a defendant brave enough to assert his rights? Is that subsequent confession truly voluntary, and a knowing and intelligent relinquishment, of a known right and privilege?

Ron paused for a moment. The whispering from some of the spectators was enough to answer his questions in the otherwise quiet courtroom. He had made his point. Looking into the eyes of the justices said it all. They were sitting back in their big leather chairs and it was easy to see that their minds were answering the questions Ron had just posed.

Finished with his argument, Ron thanked the justices, packed up his notes, and headed out of the chambers with me trailing close behind. On the plane ride back home, both of us sat quietly with our own thoughts about the experience. For me, getting to know

Mattson through the trial transcripts and exhibits was more than enough. Halfway through the material I had read, sitting in my living room, I remembered being completely repulsed by his cavalier attitude toward his victims. These were young girls just beginning life, and they were brutally assaulted by an individual with no conscience. What person with a conscience wouldn't have second thoughts about helping someone like Mattson? While I had second thoughts earlier in the trial, I had to ignore his behavior and concentrate on his defense, and now we were finally finished. I could go back to leading my life without Mattson being part of it.

I closed my eyes and went to sleep.

ELEVEN

REVERSAL

It took the California Supreme Court two years to render its decision. On October 22, 1984, the justices reversed Michael Dee Mattson's conviction.

I am quite sure there are moments in each of our lives that we can recall years later with the utmost clarity. To this day, I can remember the exact details of the call I received from Ron announcing the California Supreme Court's decision. At the time, I had moved on with my life and, quite frankly, was not even consciously aware of the pending decision. The justices had taken so long from the moment the appellate brief had been submitted and argued that in the corresponding time, my second son, Jamayne, was born, we had moved to a new house, and my professional career was starting to take off.

"Jim, are you sitting down?" These words from Ron were all too familiar.

"I am now," I replied, recognizing the excitement in Ron's voice and taking a seat in anticipation of his news.

"The California Supreme Court has just reversed Mattson's conviction!"

For the moment I was stunned, not for the verdict's favorable rendering, but for the fact that the decision was finally in and that that chapter of my life was closed at last. I was relieved that it was over. My thoughts were interrupted by Ron.

"Jim, say *something*!"

"Congratulations," was all I could muster.

"To both of us," Ron replied.

"What was the basis of the decision?" I asked after gathering my wits.

"Well, honestly, the decision embraces the issues you brought up regarding Dingle's failure to cease all interrogations once Mattson asserted his rights the first time. They also determined that Dingle was basically held to the same standards as California law enforcement personnel, because the California Constitution applied to Mattson as a citizen, regardless of the law enforcement agency conducting the interrogation."

From a professional standpoint, I was very happy. To be proven right under the circumstances gave me a fantastic feeling, especially since the decision focused on the issues I had brought to Ron's attention. Ron and I briefly discussed our mutual excitement over having accomplished such a feat, and we ended our conversation with plans to celebrate. I didn't say anything to Ron, but after hearing the news, I was concerned about how Betty would react to it. Clearly, she was not going to be happy, given our previous discussions. Two years had passed and the subject rarely, if ever, came up between us. Honestly, I did not want to shake things up by bringing up an issue that no longer affected us directly.

Betty had been present when I received the call from Ron, so I knew that evading the problem altogether was out of the question. I had been married long enough to know I wasn't going to be able to put it off. After hanging up the phone, I said nothing and continued working on a salad, which was my contribution toward the evening meal. The silence was broken by Betty, asking a question to which she already knew the answer.

"So, who was that?"

"Oh, it was Ron. He said to give you his best," I replied in a nonchalant manner.

"Is that *why* he called?" She had a look on her face that required me to tell her the truth.

There was no avoiding what would be a long discussion. I set aside my bowl and told Betty the California Supreme Court had reversed Mattson's conviction, but I neglected to give her any details that directly linked me to the decision. At that moment, of course, I had not read the actual decision, and I wanted to completely understand what the court actually said before entering into an in-depth conversation that would only rehash old sentiments.

"*Reversed the decision!*" In a tone that was less than cordial, Betty challenged me. "Why would they want that animal back out on the streets?" she said, pulling out a chair in our small breakfast nook. I followed her, sighing.

"Betty, you have to understand that the justices do not make decisions based on personal feelings or emotions. Their job is to objectively consider all of the facts, and apply those facts to legal principles. If the decision turns in favor of a person like Mattson, so be it!"

"And what about you, Jimi? How do *you* feel about a decision like that—when *you* were basically responsible for it?"

As I stared at Betty, it was very clear to me that her concern was not the justices' reasoning, but rather the fact that I had helped a sexual predator and serial killer escape justice. I was not in a position to answer her question, and made that point obvious by my silence.

TWELVE

THE COURT'S DECISION

After two years of waiting, with the decision finally in and Mattson's conviction overturned, I was very interested to read and analyze the Court's decision. After I received my copy of the decision from Ron, we discussed the holding in some detail. We celebrated the victory over dinner with our wives, Jennifer and Betty. I knew that Betty was not interested in participating in the festivities, as her viewpoint was contrary to the decision. Yet she came along because she knew it was expected of her. Jennifer, on the other hand, was formerly a court reporter, and as the wife of a well-established attorney, did not get emotionally attached to such matters.

Although I never received any official credit for my involvement in the court's decision, it nevertheless constituted a defining moment in my life. As such, I wanted to clearly understand the court's rationale in reversing Mattson's conviction.

Upon reading the opinions, I was glad to see that the key facts the justices mentioned were consistent with certain details Ron and I had focused on in our arguments, which probably differed from the key facts that the prosecution would have focused on in their arguments.

The key points focused on the fact that Dingle, although technically a detective in Nevada, appeared to be working for the California law enforcement agencies while he was interviewing Mattson about the Kiz Livingston case.

In rendering its decision to overturn Mattson's conviction, the Court emphasized that:

> Officer Dingle repeatedly questioned defendant on "a number of areas," each time advising him of his rights; most of these conversations were initiated by Dingle and all seem to have taken place in the

absence of counsel. Throughout this period Dingle kept in close contact with various California Law enforcement agencies.

The Court also focused on the fact that the California detectives questioned Mattson without Mattson's attorney being in the room with them. In its decision, the Court said:

On November 7, 1978, Officer Reed of the Los Angeles Police Department went to North Las Vegas to question the defendant about the death of Cheryl G. He first spoke with Officer Dingle, who informed him that when defendant was arrested in Ely he had invoked his privilege against self-incrimination and had asked for counsel. Reed then asked Dingle to contact the Nevada Public Defender—not, he testified, to secure counsel's consent to the questioning, but merely to inform him of the interrogation as a matter of "courtesy" or "protocol." Dingle telephoned the Public Defender's Office but was unable to reach the defendant's lawyer at that time; he made no attempt to speak with his supervisor, but instead left a message for the attorney.

The Court concluded that Mattson's rights had in fact been violated, by Dingle and the Los Angeles Police Department, which is why the justices overturned the conviction, potentially releasing Mattson back onto the streets.

Reading the California Supreme Court's decision, I was highly satisfied with the results. I had done my job, and I had done it well. The Court had focused on several of the arguments I had personally come up with in making the decision it did. The fact that Mattson could possibly be free again to prey on new victims entered my mind, but I dismissed those thoughts. I had to.

THIRTEEN

THE RETRIAL

It is said that every dog has his day, and Mattson had his when the Supreme Court reversed his conviction. As was its privilege, the Los Angeles County District Attorney's office elected to retry Mattson before he was ever released from prison.

When I received the call from Ron telling me this news, he sounded quite nonchalant. We had done our job. We discussed the decision made by the DA's office and agreed that it made sense. A high-profile case such as this one demanded a second chance at obtaining a conviction, if for no other reason than at a minimum Mattson would remain behind bars until the trial was over and all appeals had been exhausted. That process could conceivably take years.

After I hung up with Ron, I reflected upon my personal feelings about this decision. I was very glad, professionally speaking, that I had done my part. But the haunting feelings of my sister's circumstances, and of the young victims brutalized by Mattson, began to resurface.

My involvement with Mattson's appeal appeared to be never ending. I had thought that I could let it go, but I was having trouble. What was it about this man? Why did my life have to be touched by him? I began to wonder whether or not he was truly sorry for the crimes he had committed against those young girls. Probably not. I wondered how he took the news of the Supreme Court's ruling. He was probably up at San Quentin celebrating with his fellow inmates, with each one asking how he pulled it off in the desperate hope that he had some magical answer on how they could also escape death.

I found myself thinking about it too much. This bothered me. I was becoming preoccupied with wondering about whether Mattson would get out. Maybe I was bothered because at one time I viewed him as the same type of individual that assaulted my sister.

I was happy Mattson was not going to be released. I began to wonder, professionally speaking, how the DA could possibly get another conviction since the confessions had been deemed inadmissible. I had to wait approximately one year, but my question was finally answered. On December 10, 1985, Mattson was retried in the Norwalk Superior Court. Less than two weeks later, jurors, after deliberating for a mere two hours, again convicted Mattson and recommended death in the gas chamber. On February 7, 1986, Judge Thomas F. Nuss formally sentenced him to die for the strangulation slayings of Cheryl Gutierrez and Adele Jean Corradini. With that formal sentence, Mattson once more became entitled to an automatic appeal to the California Supreme Court. He'd come full circle.

The judicial system afforded Mattson another opportunity to have his conviction set aside. This time, the wheels of justice turned a lot more slowly. It would be four years before Mattson would learn his fate. On May 3, 1990, twelve years after his victims had been laid to rest, Mattson was informed that the California Supreme Court justices had affirmed his conviction, which would ultimately mean his death.

Over the years, I never actually kept up with what was going on with Mattson's case because, quite frankly, I had too many other things going on in my life. Yet in February 2005, prompted by the growing number of sexual predator abductions in the news, those old feelings started returning. My thoughts drifted back to my involvement with Mattson. I called Ron to see if he had ever heard anything more about Mattson. Several days later, I received a copy of the May 3, 1990, California Supreme Court decision in the mail.

In reconvicting Mattson, the justices explained their decision:

> The Court believes that the jury's verdict as to the death penalty in the penalty phase is definitely supported by the evidence. And the Court has and does make an independent determination that it is so supported.

> The court has also considered the argument of counsel that the death penalty is wrong and that government should not participate in taking another life, the fact that the defendant may have been seriously mentally ill or is, in fact, seriously

mentally ill, and the court must make a determination as to his moral culpability.

We are not perfect. This court is not perfect. But we do the very best we possibly can under the circumstances. And if we don't attempt to do that, it's just anarchy. And this court is not going to participate in that. Each one of us ha[s] to be responsible for those acts we commit. And I believe Mr. Mattson should be responsible for the acts he commits.

I agree with counsel that some people may wish to take the life of another out of revenge or fear. I have no great joy in being here and having to listen to what Mr. Mattson participated in, nor do I believe either counsel had any great love of being here during the course of this trial.

The fact of the matter is, that's our job. And I believe that Mr. Mattson is definitely legally responsible under the law for his acts and should be so punished. And insofar as this court or anyone is able to do so, he is probably morally culpable for it. But I can't make those judgments any more than anyone else can. Someone else is going to make those judgments.

But I do not believe that Mattson was seriously mentally ill under the law at the time of those offenses. I don't know what kind of person does the type of things that Mr. Mattson does. But the evidence is abundantly, convincingly clear that he did it. And under the law, he should be punished.

The Court has considered the fact that each of these crimes, each of them, involved great bodily harm, each one.

Each one indicated a high degree of cruelty and viciousness in almost every instance, not the least of which the 9-year-old-girl.

But in each instance the victims were particularly vulnerable. All of his crimes have involved multiple victims. Each crime was carried out with premeditation. He has engaged in a pattern of violent conduct for many years prior to these offenses in 1978, which indicates he is a serious danger to society.

He has served prison terms. He was on parole when he committed the offenses for which he was tried.

The Court, in attempting to look at any circumstance in mitigation and reviewing the testimony that was presented at the time of the penalty phase of this case, the Court, in considering that testimony that was presented by the defendant, does not believe that any of those circumstances mitigate against the imposition of the penalty that this court intends to impose.

The Court has exercised its discretion. It has made an independent judgment. [It d]enies the defendant's motion to modify the sentence of the jury.

FOURTEEN

LIVING IN THE "Q"

And what about Michael Dee Mattson? What was he doing while legal minds debated and determined his future? He took up residence at San Quentin, a California state prison located on 432 acres on Point Quentin in Marin County, just north of San Francisco. It was opened in July 1852, is the oldest prison in California, and borders on 275 acres of waterfront that overlooks the San Francisco Bay. Estimated to be worth between $80 and $100 million, it is considered the most valuable prison in the world.

Mattson officially entered the "Q" on April 14, 1980. There are only six other condemned men who have been on death row longer than Mattson. In terms of the date of the committed offenses, only one prisoner, Douglas Stankewitz, has seniority over Mattson, and his crimes were committed only five months before Mattson committed his crimes. There are currently 666 condemned men on death row and life there is anything but glamorous. There he sits, along with his fellow inmates, year after year, waiting to die either by the executioner, disease, natural causes, or even suicide if he can no longer take the pressure and can figure out how to do it successfully, as twelve others have done before him.

The prison consists of concrete floors, clanging cell doors, and a lime green execution chamber, which was converted from a gas-style death chamber to a room that accommodates the more commonly used lethal injection method. Two chairs once sat where the restraining table is now located. Only eleven people have met their deaths there since 1978, and nine of those were executed by lethal injection since 1995. Mattson, having arrived in 1980, came at the right time. In the early 1980s, in response to a federal motion filed by condemned prisoners, San Quentin officials signed a consent decree agreeing to provide certain living conditions specifically for the men on death row.

How does Mattson spend his time? Mattson begins his day by being served breakfast from a hot cart. The guard basically shovels the food onto paper trays, and shoves it into the cell. Dinner is served the same way, but lunch is simpler. It is not served hot like the other two meals, and consists of sandwiches, fruit, and chips all served in a paper bag.

After breakfast, he gets released to head out to the yard for five hours per day, first being subject to a strip search to ensure that he as well as his fellow inmates are not carrying drugs or weapons. Each inmate is then escorted down a concrete walkway that leads out to the yard. Mattson's whole distance of travel is under the watchful eye of a guard standing on a catwalk and armed with a mini-14 rifle that has, on occasion, found its deadly mark with other inmates.

And the yard? There are six yards, and each is so small and narrow one would think they are used for dog runs. These areas are not side-by-side. They are separated from each other by two sets of chain-linked fences with a no-man's land between them. On any given day, fifty or sixty men can be crammed into any one area. Of course, while Mattson is in the yard, he has access to basketball courts, weight-lifting equipment, jump ropes, heavy ropes, and heavy bags for working out.

Also at San Quentin, Mattson is allowed to participate in educational programs and arts and crafts, and there are telephones on each tier of the facility so he can make collect phone calls to his family, friends, and attorney. He even has access to the Internet.

Within the granite walls of San Quentin, there are actually three death rows. A fourth is located at the California Institute for Women in Frontera. There are only a few women housed at that facility, each awaiting any word that her conviction has been overturned.

Although Mattson would love to be housed in the "North Seg," which is considered the luxury penthouse suite, housing the likes of Charles Manson, Sirhan Sirhan, and other infamous criminals, he is instead housed in "East Block," designated as "Death Row II," a huge warehouse-type building that also provides shelter to various kinds of birds that have found security from predators within the walls of San Quentin. East Block was built in 1927. There are two sides to East Block, the Bay-side and the Yard-side. Each side has five tiers of fifty-four cells, which house approximately two hundred and fifty condemned men.

At San Quentin, any prisoner stepping out of line gets sent to the Adjustment Center, where condemned men are housed and counseled so that they can learn to cope with the brutal realities of living day-to-day on death row. Mattson has spent his prison life in the Adjustment Center since 1993. He has been assaulted and spat upon by other inmates, not only because he killed a child, but also because they blame him for the three strikes law in California, which requires mandatory jail time for those convicted of serious criminal offenses on three separate occasions.

Does Mattson sit by, watching the clock tick down the minutes to his impending date with the executioner? Not a chance. Most death row inmates in San Quentin become jailhouse lawyers very quickly. They exchange legal strategies and read as much as they can about the law. They have access to all their court records free of cost. They can get their court transcripts, copies of exhibits, copies of depositions, and have unlimited access to their attorneys. They file appeal after appeal after appeal until they have exhausted the appeals process. This is why it normally takes so long to execute condemned inmates in California.

And what are the living victims and the families of the murdered victims doing? Trying to put their lives in order and keeping up with the status of the legal proceedings that will hopefully help them bring some closure to their lives. It's about all that they can do.

Closure for Mattson might come by execution or by his death from some other method. He knows it's just a matter of time before he eats his last meal and then takes those traditional thirteen steps between his cell and the lime green chamber.

AFTERWORD

The judicial process is made up of legal principles, opinions, and arguments. The Mattson case is a prime example of this statement. In the first appeal, Ron and I had a difference of opinion based upon facts and legal principles. The justices involved in the first and second California Supreme Court appeals also had differences of opinion.

Mattson has learned to manipulate the system. Taking advantage of the judicial process, he has filed yet another appeal. This one, however, appears to be his last major appeal. On June 28, 1996, he filed his second amended petition to the United States District Court, Central District of California. This particular appeal is a habeas corpus appeal, which contains a petition to the federal district court that alleges he is being illegally held by the state of California. This particular appeal has literally taken ten years to be resolved. It contains sixty claims about Mattson's supposed rights that have been violated from the moment he was arrested through the trial and appeal processes.

His federal public defender, Linda L. Griffis, has skillfully represented him throughout the entire process. When I started this project, I contacted her for permission to write to Mattson, which she gave. In my correspondence to him, I introduced myself and explained how I had assisted Ron in his appeal so many years before. I asked him if there were any statements or information that he would like for me to include in this book. In my letter, I made it perfectly clear that I did not expect him to give me any information that would jeopardize his appeal. Unfortunately, he was not very obliging. He's still hanging on to hope. What do any of the death row inmates have but hope in their small world of hopelessness? Each passing day brings them closer to the day they will have to die.

It is insignificant whether we as a society agree or disagree with the courts' decisions that put these individuals where they are. Mattson is where he is because of his own actions. These circumstances are emotional for all of us as a whole.

I can personally agree with Justice Mosk and Justice Broussard because their position was consistent with mine during the first appeal. There was an obvious change on the high court before the second appeal, however, with key justices being replaced. I can now appreciate the amount of controversy surrounding President George W. Bush's selections for the United States Supreme Court. Such changes to the political makeup of the Supreme Court could have a significant impact on future decisions they render, especially with regard to the death penalty and allowable methods of execution.

On November 4, 1986, under California's unusual judicial-retention election system—it's one of the few states that grants voters the choice to keep or oust their Supreme Court justices, whereas in other states, the justices are in for life—the voters removed Bird, Grodin, and Reynoso from their seats on the high court. These three justices' liberal views toward the imposition of the death penalty directly affected the voters' decision to oust them. As a result of the election and the antiliberal campaign against Bird herself, then-governor George Deukmejian, a law-and-order Republican, was placed in a position to appoint three new justices whose views were considered conservative and who would move the high court in a more right-leaning and pro–death penalty direction. Sitting justice Malcolm Lucas was appointed the new chief justice to take Bird's place.

As you already know, Mattson's second appeal was decided in May 1990. The justices deciding the merits of his case were probably already poised to render decisions contrary to the Bird Court, which had originally overturned Mattson's conviction.

On another note, society has a bigger problem with which it has not adequately dealt. Sexual predators continue to stalk, kidnap, rape, and murder our children. Some that are captured and imprisoned are eventually released with no signs of having been rehabilitated, like Mattson after his first incarceration.

Mattson's long journey through the judicial process is nearing its end. On November 28, 2007, the Court, after ten years of needless motions, petitions, requests for extensions, and every stall tactic available, rendered an unfavorable determination that all but clears the way for Mattson's execution. In essence, Mattson has exhausted his legal appeals.

Mattson, in all likelihood, has a debt that can never be fully repaid, whether or not he makes it to his execution date. (Rumor has it that he may have some major health issues that might cause his demise prior to his date with destiny.) Only time will tell. While Mattson will have spent these many years in prison, even with his execution, his victims can never be made whole again; their families can never fully heal.

Betty and I eventually divorced, but we have maintained an excellent relationship. During the process of writing this book, I have been asked on a number of occasions whether or not my involvement in the Mattson case was the beginning of the end for Betty and me. Who knows? When marriages end, the breakup is usually based on a number of factors, not merely a single issue, and it is seldom caused by any one person. What we had for as long as we had it was something special. The reasons we separated do not matter now. We have two sons together who continue to make us proud every day. Jamal is married and has given us three wonderful grandchildren, and Jamayne is getting ready to graduate from college and may play professional basketball overseas. They are the real tribute to our relationship.

As for me, I never went into criminal law, but pursued a career representing employers in the employment law arena instead. I have a very successful business, and often think about what it took to attain my level of achievement. Mental discipline and an attitude not to accept defeat have been key components. Another important factor was the support I received, and continue to receive, from my current wife Brenda, who was introduced to me by a mutual client. She has been an integral part of my success as a person, as well as my success as a businessperson. She encouraged me to write this book and bring closure to my feelings about the events surrounding my sister and my involvement with Mattson's case. Our relationship is truly a validation that the second time around can be fantastic.

As I close, I want it to be perfectly understood that when I reflect back on the Mattson appeal, I have no regrets as to my involvement. I find comfort knowing that I did my job—Mattson was given his right to counsel. My position after all these years remains the same. We live in a society that has set a certain standard, well-established by the U.S. Constitution, state constitutions, and legal precedents that have been and will continue to be established by case law. We have to understand that every individual who is arrested for a crime, no matter its heinousness, is entitled to certain protections that cannot be overlooked based upon emotions—those of society, the police, the lawyers who defend and prosecute the accused, and finally, the judges who hear the case. If we fail to recognize this basic truth, the victims of such crimes will not have their right of vindication in a judicial system designed specifically for that purpose. We must keep the focus and remember that it's not a matter of choice, but a matter of rights, not just for those of the suspect, but for those of the victim as well. Justice must always be served.